Behavior Modification

Managing Behavior Series

Behavior Modification: Basic Principles
The Measurement of Behavior

BEHAVIOR MODIFICATION

Basic Principles

Third Edition

David L. Lee
Saul Axelrod

pro·ed
An International Publisher

8700 Shoal Creek Boulevard
Austin, Texas 78757-6897
800/897-3202   Fax 800/397-7633
www.proedinc.com

© 2005, 1999, 1975, 1971 by PRO-ED, Inc.
8700 Shoal Creek Boulevard
Austin, Texas 78757-6897
800/897-3202   Fax 800/397-7633
www.proedinc.com

Library of Congress Cataloging-in-Publication Data

Lee, David L.
    Behavior modification : basic principles—3rd ed. / David L. Lee, Saul Axelrod.
        p. cm.
    Second ed. by Saul Axelrod and R. Vance Hall.
    Includes bibliographical references (p.   ).
    ISBN-13: 978-141640058-5
    ISBN-10: 1-4164-0058-3 (softcover : alk. paper)
    1. Behavior Modification.   I. Axelrod, Saul.   II. Axelrod, Saul. Behavior Modification
III. Title.

BF637.B4A94 2005
153.8'5—dc22

                                                                        2004062484

This book is designed in Minion and Gill Sans.

Printed in the United States of America

    3   4   5   6   10   09   08   07

CONTENTS

PREFACE

The original Managing Behavior series was published in 1969. At that time few texts were available to introduce students to what was then called behavior modification and is now usually referred to as applied behavior analysis. The original series contained three parts: *The Measurement of Behavior, Basic Principles,* and *Applications in School and Home.* Since that first edition some 35 years ago, the series has been revised and *Applications in School and Home* has been discontinued. This book provided examples of behavior analysis studies carried out by parents and teachers. Today many such studies that demonstrate the application of behavior principles across various settings are available in the literature, something that was not true when the original edition was published.

Since their first publication, more than 300,000 copies each of *The Measurement of Behavior* and *Basic Principles* have been sold; they have been translated into Spanish, Portuguese, Hebrew, Dutch, and French. Thousands of students and practitioners have received their first introductions to behavior analysis through these books. The books are still being widely used because the information is presented in a simple, straightforward, and easy-to-understand manner.

The approach in the first of this two-part series, *The Measurement of Behavior,* teaches readers to observe and measure behaviors that they wish to change as simply as possible. The second part, *Basic Principles,* presents the basic principles of behavior, emphasizing the use of preventive, or antecedent, techniques as well as consequences naturally available in the home, business, or school environment to change important behaviors. This approach differs from some behavioral models

that stress the use of complex graphing of data, extrinsic reinforcers, and complicated reinforcer systems and equipment.

This revised edition of *Behavior Modification: Basic Principles* has been expanded to provide clearer and more compre-
hensive examples for the reader. A new section on functional assessment and a step-by-step guide for developing behavior change
programs have been added. The theme of the book, however, has
not changed in more than 30 years. Behavior occurs for a reason, and that reason can be found in the environment.

The authors are indebted to the many students, teachers,
parents, and others who helped develop these materials and to
the many people who have shared with us their experiences in
the successful application of behavior management techniques
in home, school, work, and community environments. We are
further indebted to Chris Ann Worsham of PRO-ED, who provided assistance and encouragement on this revision.

INTRODUCTION

You have probably observed this scenario a hundred times: A parent and child are moving through the checkout at the local grocery. With seemingly impeccable timing the child begins to ask for candy. There is no escape. The parent knows it. The child knows it. The groceries are on the conveyer and an impatient-looking person has pulled her cart into the same checkout line behind the pair. The child starts off by sheepishly pointing to the candy. However, when the parent refuses to make the purchase, the child systematically ratchets up the volume and intensity of the request until he is in a tantrum. At this point, the embarrassed parent grabs the candy from the display, tosses it onto the conveyer, and somehow rationalizes the purchase (e.g., "You were good for most of the shopping trip").

As parents and teachers we may ask, "Why?" Why did the child begin to cry at that particular time? Why did the parent purchase the candy? What would have happened if the parent had refused? What could the parent do to make the checkout less stressful next time? All these excellent questions relate to the purpose of this book. As shown by this familiar example, the principles of behavior operate all around us, from the father who purchases candy for the crying child in the checkout line, to a teacher who praises a correct answer, to the supervisor who rewards hard work. We can choose to ignore these principles and allow behavior to develop in a random fashion, or we can use them to help change behaviors with social and personal relevance.

Changing behavior is a complex process and requires specialized knowledge and skills. However, when you boil all of this knowledge and skill down, you have two major questions: Why does a behavior occur, and how can I change this behavior?

Conceptually, there are two major sections of this book. The first addresses why individuals engage in certain behavior. This "why" question is linked directly to behavior principles and theory. Without knowing why behaviors occur, you will never be able to affect lasting change on those behaviors. The second section provides a series of steps that teachers and parents can use to implement formal behavior change programs to address the "how" question. Let's start our discussion by examining two types of behavior.

Two Types of Behavior: Respondent and Operant

Behavior refers to anything a person does. Driving to work, eating a sandwich, and completing a math problem are all examples of behavior. B. F. Skinner (1938), the modern founder of behavior analysis, noted that there are two types of behavior. The first is called *respondent behavior* and refers to reflexive or involuntary behavior. Examples include perspiring in the presence of heat and salivating in the presence of food. Respondent behaviors are elicited, meaning automatic, such as heat automatically causing perspiration and food automatically causing salivation.

Operant behaviors, on the other hand, are voluntary behaviors. Examples include a father carrying his daughter on his shoulders, a student raising his or her hand in class, and a person working on a computer. Operant behavior was so named because it operates on, or affects, the environment. The environment, in turn, operates on or affects the behavior in some manner. Operant behaviors are emitted, unlike respondent behaviors, which are elicited.

Causes of Respondent and Operant Behavior

The term *stimuli* refers to objects or events in the environment that change behavior. Some stimuli come before a behavior, and some come after a behavior. Respondent behaviors are controlled by stimuli that precede the behavior. Thus, heat precedes perspiration and food precedes salivation. The stimuli that elicit respondent behaviors are known as *unconditioned stimuli*. Operant behaviors, on the other hand, are controlled by stimuli that follow the behavior. Thus, praise or criticism following a behavior will likely change the probability that a behavior will occur again in similar situations. These stimuli are called *consequent stimuli*, or more simply, *consequences*.

Conditioning

Behaviors occur because they have been conditioned. Conditioning refers to a process by which behavior is changed by environmental stimuli. These environmental stimuli increase or decrease the chances that a behavior will occur. Both respondent and operant behaviors can be conditioned. However, the method of conditioning for both types of behaviors differs.

Respondent Conditioning

It is possible for a neutral stimulus to acquire the ability to elicit a respondent behavior. The process, first identified by Russian physiologist Ivan Pavlov in his work with dogs, is known as *respondent* or *classical conditioning* (Schwartz, 1978). Pavlov noted that a bell was originally neutral in its ability to produce salivation from a dog (i.e., the bell alone did not elicit salivation). Yet when the bell was repeatedly presented shortly before food was introduced, the dog salivated simply from the presentation of the bell. Thus, the bell acquired the capacity to elicit salivation and was called a *conditioned stimulus*. Of course, when Pavlov presented only the bell and not the food, the bell eventually lost its ability to elicit salivation, a process identified as *respondent extinction*.

Emotional behavior is respondent behavior. When emotional behavior occurs in the classroom, in the home, or on the job, it can interfere with learning and performance. Stimuli associated with powerful punishers often elicit strong emotional responses. Take Francine, for example, who is a student in Mr. W's class. During group oral reading, Mr. W embarrasses Francine by making sarcastic remarks about her lack of reading fluency. After repeated criticism, Francine begins to associate the embarrassing remarks with reading class. Now when Francine comes to reading group her stomach begins to cramp, her mouth becomes dry, and her palms start to sweat. These emotional responses, elicited by reading, complete a circle of academic difficulties for Francine. What started as a few seemingly innocuous remarks by a teacher result in Francine actively avoiding oral reading. In trying to prevent the anxiety associated with oral reading, Francine has made it highly unlikely that she will become fluent in this very important skill. When teachers use criticism, ridicule, sarcasm, or physical punishment, they are likely to elicit emotional responses. In addition, because of respondent conditioning, the activity, the classroom, and the teacher, all of which are frequently paired with these stimuli, may come to elicit emotional responses. Thus, for these children, even coming into the presence of the teacher or being told that it is time for a given activity may result in emotional behavior that will interfere with learning. To prevent this, or to overcome the situation once it has occurred, educators need to make certain that criticism and other forms of punishment are not paired with a school setting for a considerable period. Better yet, praise for appropriate behavior can replace criticism for inappropriate behavior.

Operant Conditioning

Operant conditioning refers to the process by which the consequences of behavior change the future rate of the behavior. The *law of effect* provides the basis for operant conditioning. This law states that pleasant consequences make a behavior more likely to occur in the future. Similarly, unpleasant consequences make it less likely that a behavior will occur in the future. For example, if a student volunteers an answer in class and receives a teacher's compliment, the student is likely to answer more questions in the future. On the other hand, if that same student receives a sarcastic comment or is ignored, she or he may be less willing to volunteer answers or comments in the future.

Reinforcement

Reinforcement is the most pervasive principle of behavior. It is the process by which the consequences of a behavior increase the future rate of that behavior. In other words, a person performs a behavior and experiences a consequence. If the behavior occurs more frequently in the future than it did in the past, reinforcement is said to have occurred. For example, if a mother makes a deal with her teenage son that she will pay him to mow the lawn and then he does so more frequently in the future, the mother has used a reinforcement procedure.

Often a person cannot tell whether something is a reinforcer until she or he tries it out. First, the person notes how often the behavior occurred under normal, or *baseline*, conditions. Then she or he tries out the potential reinforcement procedure. Only if the behavior increased in rate could the person say that reinforcement occurred. Take Tory as an example. Tory rarely volunteers information during class discussions in social studies. Her teacher first collects baseline data on the number of times Tory volunteers information. As shown on the graph (see Figure 1), the number of comments is very low. After collecting baseline data, the teacher begins to give bonus points for comments. However, in this case bonus points do not act as a reinforcer. It is only after the teacher begins giving verbal praise that Tory's class participation increases. In this case verbal praise acts as a reinforcer to increase Tory's class participation.

> **KEY TERM:** *Reinforcement*
> Process by which consequences of a behavior increase the probability that the behavior will occur in the future.

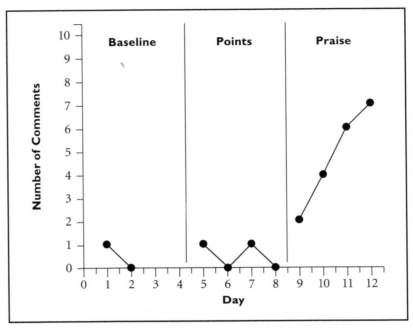

Figure 1. The effects of various consequences on Tory's behavior.

The Effectiveness of Reinforcement Programs

It is not uncommon to hear someone say, "Oh, I tried reinforcement, and that stuff doesn't work." Fortunately, some guidelines can help make reinforcement programs more effective.
When designing a reinforcement program, practitioners should
be aware that (a) delivering reinforcers immediately after the
target behavior, (b) delivering reinforcers only when the target
behavior occurs (i.e., contingently), and (c) varying the type of
reinforcers all affect the outcome of programs.

Immediacy of Reinforcement

Reinforcement must immediately follow the desired behavior in
order to have its maximum effect. It is important to deliver a
reinforcer immediately after a targeted behavior occurs because
that behavior will then become most closely associated with
the reinforcer. If reinforcement is delayed, the consequences

might become associated with a different behavior. For example, Mr. V observes Jim engage in an appropriate prosocial behavior (e.g., saying "Thank you"). Instead of immediately reinforcing the appropriate behavior, Mr. V waits until the end of class. Figure 2 shows the events pictorially.

However, Jim is likely to engage in many behaviors between the initial prosocial behavior and the delivery of the reinforcer. By delaying the delivery of the reinforcer, Mr. V may have inadvertently reinforced other behaviors that may or may not be appropriate. Figure 3 shows this sequence pictorially.

So, teachers who move around the classroom and immediately compliment correct answers are more effective than teachers who stay in one place. Bonuses for outstanding performance should be given out daily or weekly rather than annually. Parents who use toys as reinforcers for weekly improvement in school should have the toys available at the end of the week, rather than purchasing them on the weekend.

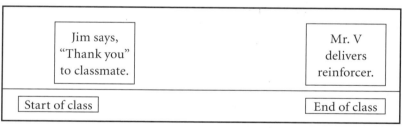

Figure 2. Diagram of delay of reinforcement for Jim.

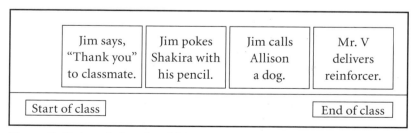

Figure 3. Unintended results of delaying reinforcement for Jim.

▶ **Assignment:** Suggest how the following people might more immediately reinforce behavior than is commonly the case.

1. A parent ————————————————

2. A teacher ————————————————

3. An employer ————————————————

4. Yourself ————————————————

Reinforcement Must Be Contingent

An increase in pay will not necessarily make employees more productive. Similarly, giving students extra free time will not automatically get them to work harder. If reinforcement is such a good procedure, why do these reinforcers not always work? What is missing is that the bonuses are not *contingent* on the target behavior. A contingent relationship is an if–then relationship. If the desired behavior occurs, then the reinforcer will be delivered. The delivery of a reinforcer must be contingent on the desired behavior in order to increase the future likelihood of that behavior. Thus, increases in pay must be contingent on increased employee productivity, and extra free time must be contingent on appropriate student behavior.

▶ **Assignment:** A mother says to her daughter, "As soon as you are done calling your friends, I want you to set the table and do your homework." What should the mother be saying to increase homework completion?

————————————————————

————————————————————

Varying the Reinforcers

If someone uses the same reinforcer over and over again, the reinforcer may lose its value. When using reinforcement procedures, it is better to use a variety of reinforcers. For example, when delivering compliments, a person can use expressions such as "Very good," "Wonderful," "Nicely done," and "I am really impressed." Parents can treat their children to a movie on one occasion and a trip to a sporting event on another. When employers give their staff a financial bonus, a variety of reinforcers are inherent, because money can be used to purchase a multitude of items.

A person's receptivity to a reinforcer is different at different times. Thus, a person who enters a health club might rush to an open treadmill, but 30 minutes later, after the person has completed his or her workout, the treadmill is of no appeal. Similarly, a child who has unlimited access to television will not work for the opportunity to watch television. Limiting the ordinary availability of a potential reinforcer is an important factor in creating its appeal.

Basic Principles Quiz 1

1. Define *stimulus*.

_____

_____

_____

_____

_____

_____

2. In respondent behavior, does a stimulus precede or follow a response?

_____

_____

3. What are two differences between respondent and operant behaviors?

   _____

   _____

   _____

   _____

   _____

4. Respondent conditioning occurs when we repeatedly pair a neutral stimulus with an unconditioned stimulus until the neutral stimulus

   _____ .

5. Respondent extinction occurs when the conditioned stimulus is presented repeatedly

   _____ .

6. If school has been repeatedly paired with stimuli that elicit strong undesirable emotional responses, what needs to be done?

   _____

   _____

   _____

   _____

7. Define and give an example of *operant conditioning*.

   _____

   _____

   _____

   _____

8. Define *reinforcement*.

_____

_____

_____

_____

_____

_____

_____

_____

9. To maximize the effectiveness of a reinforcement procedure, the following three conditions must be met:

   a. _____

   _____

   b. _____

   _____

   c. _____

   _____

10. Give everyday examples of how reinforcement is used in
    the following environments:

    a. Home _____

    _____

    b. School _____

    _____

    c. Work _____

    _____

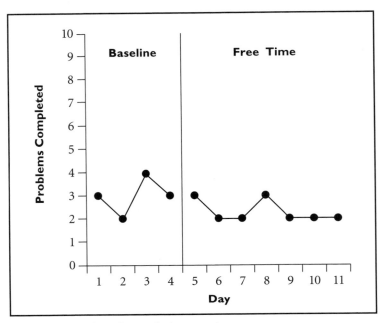

Figure 4. Stacy's work completion over time.

11. Mr. C gives Stacy free time contingent on math problem completion. Use the graph in Figure 4 to determine whether free time acted as a reinforcer for problem completion. Why or why not?

_____

_____

_____

_____

_____

REINFORCEMENT OPERATIONS

There are two types of reinforcement operations: positive and negative. Both types have the effect of increasing the probability of the behavior that precedes the reinforcer. Negative reinforcement should not be confused with punishment, which is described later in this book (see "Procedures for Decreasing Behavior").

Positive Reinforcement

In a *positive reinforcement* operation, a person performs a behavior and then something that person likes is presented. If the future rate of that behavior increases, positive reinforcement has occurred. Examples of this procedure are endless: a baby smiling at his parents when he is picked up; a teacher praising his class for working quietly during study period; a child thanking a parent for buying candy at the store; and a mother giving an extra 5 dollars in allowance when her son helps around the house. What differentiates a positive reinforcer from a neutral stimulus in each of these situations is that the target behavior (e.g., picking up the baby, working quietly during study period, buying candy, and helping around the house) increases over time.

Employers, parents, teachers, and children who have learned to deliver positive reinforcers are generally more successful at changing behavior over the long term than are people who do not have this skill. Because preferred items and activities have been paired with these individuals, they themselves may become a reinforcer. Unfortunately, people often resort to the age-old practice of punishing undesirable behavior instead of trying to increase appropriate behavior using positive reinforcement. The continual use of punishment can result in heightened levels of anxiety and avoidance. In a successful positive reinforcement procedure, only winners exist. People who receive positive reinforcement glow with pride and excitement. Parents, teachers, and employers feel good about themselves when they positively reinforce behavior and see favorable results.

Two Key Points About Positive Reinforcement

Before we move on, we should consider two key points regarding positive reinforcement. First, positive reinforcement can be used to increase both appropriate and inappropriate behaviors. Let us return to the example at the beginning of the book featuring a child who had a tantrum at the supermarket checkout. Parents who purchase candy in an effort to quiet their crying child may be using positive reinforcement. The chances that the child will engage in the same crying behavior during the next trip to the store are greatly enhanced when the crying is followed by preferred consequences.

Second, some authors (e.g., Kohn, 1993) have made claims that positive reinforcement undermines intrinsic motivation (i.e., performing a behavior just for the behavior's sake). The research on the effects of positive reinforcement on intrinsic motivation is equivocal. Some of the problems encountered with this research base are that intrinsic motivation is difficult to define and the consequences examined in the studies were not reinforcers (i.e., they did not increase behavior). In a recent review of this literature, Cameron, Banko, and Pierce (2001) found that (a) rewards given for low interest tasks enhanced intrinsic motivation, (b) verbal praise enhanced intrinsic motivation for high-interest tasks, and (c) intrinsic motivation decreased when rewards were expected and not tied to task performance.

Part of the argument presented by opponents of the use of positive reinforcement is based on the incorrect assumption that formal reinforcement programs, once started, must remain in effect forever. From a practical standpoint, some people may need highly structured systems of support that include parent-

or teacher-delivered reinforcers to help promote appropriate behavior. However, it is very important to fade the formal program by using more natural reinforcers. When developing a formal behavior change program, consider how to fade out the program.

> **KEY TERM:** *Positive Reinforcement*
> Positive reinforcement occurs when a person performs a behavior and receives a consequence, and then the rate of behavior increases over time.

Negative Reinforcement

When a positive reinforcement procedure is used, a person performs a behavior and receives something he or she likes. This causes the person to perform the behavior more frequently in the future. A second type of reinforcement is *negative reinforcement*. With this operation a person performs a behavior to avoid or escape something he or she dislikes. This type of reinforcement also has the effect of increasing the future rate of the behavior. Although negative reinforcement is a less obvious procedure than positive reinforcement, its occurrence is common. When a father tells his daughter that she doesn't have to help with the dishes if she finishes her peas, and then the child quickly consumes her peas, negative reinforcement has occurred. Other examples of negative reinforcement occur when a teacher tells students that they will not have homework if they finish their reading assignments on time, when a professor allows students to skip the final examination if their semester average exceeds 90%, and when a supervisor allows her employees to have a day off if all work is done early. What differentiates a negative reinforcer from a neutral stimulus in each of these situations is that the target behavior (e.g., eating peas, turning in reading assignments on time, studying, and early completion of work) increases over time. The target behaviors increased because doing the dishes, doing homework, taking the final examination, and being at work were aversive and acted as negative reinforcers. In each case these individuals engaged in a response to avoid or escape these nonpreferred tasks.

> **KEY TERM:** *Negative Reinforcement*
>
> Negative reinforcement occurs when a person performs a behavior to avoid or escape a nonpreferred situation. The result of negative reinforcement is an increase in the behavior over time.

Negative reinforcement can also produce desirable or undesirable outcomes. A desirable outcome was achieved in the case cited above when students worked hard to complete their assignments and avoided having to do homework. An undesirable example of negative reinforcement occurs when a student who dislikes group activities acts out to avoid those activities. If the teacher allows the student to avoid the group activity, for example, by sending him to time-out, she has negatively reinforced acting out and should expect the inappropriate behavior to occur in similar situations in the future. Teachers and parents must take great care not to negatively reinforce unwanted behaviors.

Although both positive and negative reinforcement operations result in increases in behavior, it is usually better to use positive reinforcement whenever possible. That is, it is better to have people work to achieve things they like rather than have them work to avoid or escape things they dislike. One problem with negative reinforcement operations is that people may sometimes avoid the entire environment in which the negative reinforcers occur. For example, a father might nag his daughter until she finishes her homework and cleans her room. One way the daughter can avoid the nagging is to finish her homework and clean her room—actions that qualify as negative reinforcement. On the other hand, the daughter can avoid the nagging simply by finding an excuse to stay away from the house. In this situation, increasing homework completion and room cleaning through positive reinforcement may provide a much more pleasant experience for father and daughter.

Sometimes it is difficult to distinguish between positive and negative reinforcement. When someone turns on a light, for example, is that person adding light (positive reinforcement) or removing darkness (negative reinforcement)? The answer is unclear and unimportant. What is important is that people use procedures to increase behavior and that, when possible, they program for the addition of pleasant consequences rather than the removal of unpleasant consequences.

Basic Principles Quiz 2

Mike appeared to be an excellent father to his new daughter, Mindy. He gave her a lot of attention and affection. Nevertheless, Mindy typically cried when she saw her father. She continued crying until her father picked her up, which he invariably did.

1. What procedure is Mindy applying to her father's behavior?

_____

2. What procedure is Mike applying to Mindy's behavior?

_____

3. How are positive reinforcement and negative reinforcement similar?

_____

_____

4. How are positive reinforcement and negative reinforcement different?

_____

_____

_____

_____

_____

5. Use the graph in Figure 5 and the following statement to determine if negative or positive reinforcement has occurred. How do you know?

Holly is sent to the office each time she throws a paper ball at another student during history class.

_____

_____

_____

_____

_____

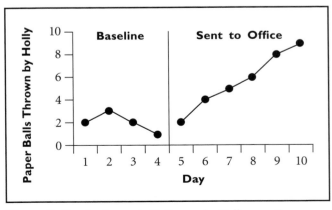

Figure 5. Graph of paper balls thrown by Holly, over time.

ESTABLISHING AND APPLYING REINFORCEMENT

Establishing Reinforcers

There is no such thing as a universal reinforcer. Some consequences will be reinforcing to some people but not to others. One student or employee might find a compliment reinforcing, whereas another might find it embarrassing or annoying. Therefore, it is important to learn how to select reinforcers and to understand how certain events become reinforcers. There are two general categories of reinforcers: primary and secondary.

Primary Reinforcers

Consequences that serve a biological need are known as *primary* or *unconditioned reinforcers*. Common primary reinforcers include food when a person is hungry, drink when a person is thirsty, sleep when a person is tired, and warmth when a person is cold. Primary reinforcers may be dependent on a state of biological deprivation, but their ability to alter behavior is genetic and is therefore not learned. A primary reinforcer does not depend on previous conditioning for its reinforcing power.

> **KEY TERM:** *Primary Reinforcers*
> Primary reinforcers are consequences that serve a biological need and are, therefore, unconditioned reinforcers.

Secondary Reinforcers

Food, drink, warmth, and sexual stimulation are important reinforcers, but they make up a small part of the consequent stimuli that reinforce behavior. In general, it is not desirable to use only primary reinforcers to change behavior. Parents, teachers, and employers do not want people to work only for food, for example, as a reinforcer. It is more desirable for people to work for consequences such as praise, attention, and merit pay. Such reinforcers are more likely to be available in the natural environment and are more socially acceptable than primary reinforcers. This second kind of reinforcer is called a *secondary* or *conditioned reinforcer* and is an event that has *acquired* its reinforcing power.

Things such as praise and money, which originally have no meaning to a person, become secondary reinforcers through the process of pairing the event with another reinforcer. For example, if a teacher gives a student a piece of candy as well as verbal praise contingent on appropriate behavior, praise will become a secondary reinforcer.

Most reinforcers available to parents, teachers, and employers are of the secondary type. It is possible to reinforce behavior with a kind word, a complimentary note, or a certificate of recognition. However, if the secondary reinforcer is no longer associated with another reinforcer, it may lose its ability to reinforce behavior. For example, if an employee keeps winning the Employee of the Month award but never gets a raise in pay, she might stop working in the manner that resulted in the award.

KEY TERM: *Secondary Reinforcers*
Secondary reinforcers are events that have acquired their reinforcing power through pairing with other established reinforcers.

▶ **Assignment:** Suppose you are the teacher or a parent of a student who is not motivated by grades. How could you make grades into conditioned reinforcers?

_____

_____

_____

_____

Individualizing Reinforcement Through Pairing

Reinforcement happens at the level of the individual. Events that are reinforcing for one person may not be reinforcing for another person. Not everyone likes apple pie, verbal praise, or trips to amusement parks.

In cases where the typical conditioned reinforcers are not effective, it may be necessary to turn to primary reinforcers or conditioned reinforcers not commonly used in a given situation. These reinforcers can then be paired with more common reinforcers, such as praise, attention, privileges, smiles, and good grades, until the latter become reinforcing. For example, sometimes it is necessary to pair verbal praise and attention with hugs, pats on the head, or even food for a child who does not initially respond to adult attention. After a time, the conditioned reinforcers will begin to take hold and physical contact and food can be reduced.

The individual nature of reinforcers is often apparent when working with children who have academic and behavioral difficulties. Often verbal praise or grades do not serve as effective reinforcers for these children because these stimuli have never been paired with other established reinforcers. What is needed is a system that supports appropriate behavior using reinforcers that, admittedly, may not be ideal in a given setting, and at the same time supports development of appropriate secondary reinforcers. After more appropriate reinforcers have been developed through systematic pairing, the initial reinforcers can be faded out.

Generalized Reinforcers

A reinforcer that has been associated with many other reinforcers is known as a *generalized conditioned reinforcer* or more simply as a *generalized reinforcer*. Praise, for example, is a generalized reinforcer for most people because it has been paired with approval, extra dessert, and raises in pay. Still, no event is a conditioned reinforcer for all people. Therefore, some people will reject praise, and some people will have no use for money reinforcers.

KEY TERM: *Generalized Reinforcer*

A generalized reinforcer is a reinforcer (e.g., praise) that has been associated with many other reinforcers (e.g., trip to favorite store, playing a game).

Deprivation and Satiation

For a reinforcer to be effective, a state of deprivation must exist for that reinforcer. For example, cheesecake can be a wonderful reinforcer; however, a person can consume only so much cheesecake. For cheesecake to act as an effective reinforcer, the person would have to be hungry for cheesecake. One reason that generalized reinforcers work so well is that they are not affected by any single state of deprivation or satiation. For example, money is still reinforcing to a person who has just seen a movie, because then money can be used to purchase a snack.

Deprivation relates to how long it has been since a reinforcer was last available. For example, a snack of milk and cookies is much more likely to be reinforcing at 4:00 P.M. than right after lunch.

Satiation occurs when too much of a given reinforcer is delivered over a short period of time. Note that a teacher who says "very good" to her students over and over may make that form of praise ineffective. In fact, some reinforcers, including food, may become unappealing if they are presented in large quantities in a short period of time. It is important to vary the type of reinforcer used and to use generalized reinforcers that do not depend on a single deprivation state in most situations. However, very few teachers, parents, or employers provide too much reinforcement. Most people err on the side of providing too little reinforcement for appropriate behavior and fail to maximize the very behavior they wish to maintain.

KEY TERM: *Deprivation*

Deprivation occurs when the person has not had access to a reinforcer for some time. Deprivation enhances the effectiveness of a reinforcer.

KEY TERM: *Satiation*

Satiation occurs when the person has had access to large quantities of a reinforcer. Satiation reduces the effectiveness of a reinforcer.

Basic Principles Quiz 3

1. Distinguish between a primary reinforcer and a secondary reinforcer.

   _____

   _____

   _____

   _____

   _____

2. Give three examples of primary reinforcers and three examples of secondary reinforcers not mentioned in this
   book.

_____

_____

_____

_____

_____

_____

3. How can a smiley face be established as a generalized reinforcer?

_____

_____

_____

_____

4. Describe a person in your environment who has a behavior in need of modification. Detail the potential steps you
   might go through to determine a reinforcer for that person's
   behavior.

_____

_____

_____

_____

5. Why is money a powerful conditioned reinforcer?

_____

_____

_____

_____

6. Define *deprivation* and *satiation*.

Schedules of Reinforcement

After deciding upon a reinforcer, one must determine how often that reinforcer should be delivered. A *schedule of reinforcement* is the pattern of timing by which reinforcers are delivered. This timing varies along a continuum from continuous reinforcement (i.e., every target response is reinforced) to extinction (i.e., a target response is never reinforced). Between these two points on the continuum are intermittent schedules. On an intermittent schedule, responses are only sometimes reinforced. Knowledge of each of the various schedules of reinforcement is important because each schedule is associated with very distinct patterns of responding. Teachers, parents, and employers can use these patterns to their advantage to design reinforcement programs to accomplish specific goals.

> **KEY TERM:** *Schedule of Reinforcement*
> A schedule of reinforcement outlines the terms under which reinforcers are delivered.

Extinction Schedules of Reinforcement

To this point most of this book has been about increasing behaviors using reinforcement. Implicit in this discussion is the understanding that for a behavior to be maintained over time it must be reinforced. In an *extinction (EXT) schedule,* reinforcers are withheld, thus decreasing the rate of behavior. An extinction schedule of reinforcement is often used to decrease maladaptive behavior. A more in-depth discussion about decreasing behaviors using extinction can be found later in this book (see "Decreasing Behavior Through Extinction").

KEY TERM: *Extinction (EXT) Schedule*

An EXT schedule is a schedule of reinforcement whereby reinforcers for a response are withheld.

Continuous Reinforcement Schedules

Continuous reinforcement (CRF) schedules result in the delivery of a reinforcer for each instance of a target behavior. This schedule generally produces a high rate of the target response, which is ideal for developing new behaviors. The high rate of responding produced by a CRF schedule is ideal for developing new behaviors because the number of learning trials that can be delivered during a fixed period increases (i.e., new behavior is performed at a higher rate). Unfortunately, some problems are associated with CRF schedules. First, CRF schedules do not produce behavior that is persistent over time. When the delivery of reinforcers stops abruptly, responding rapidly decreases. A second issue with CRF schedules is satiation. Because of the high rate of reinforcer delivery, the individual may become satiated for that reinforcer. People using a CRF schedule must vary the types of reinforcers to prevent satiation.

> **KEY TERM:** *Continuous Reinforcement (CRF) Schedule*
> A CRF schedule is a reinforcement schedule whereby every instance of a response is reinforced.

Intermittent Schedules of Reinforcement

Unlike continuous schedules, intermittent schedules reinforce only some instances of a behavior. Although there are numerous intermittent schedules of reinforcement, four are commonly used. Two are ratio schedules and two are interval schedules.

Fixed-Ratio Schedules. Reinforcers on ratio schedules are delivered contingent on a given number of responses a person has emitted. A *fixed-ratio* (FR) *schedule* designates the exact number of behaviors a person must perform in order to receive a reinforcer. On an FR 10 (i.e., fixed ratio of 10 responses) schedule, for example, a reinforcer is delivered after exactly 10 target responses occur. Using an FR 10 schedule, a teacher can offer a student 1 minute of free time for every 10 math problems the student gets correct. FR schedules produce high, steady rates of performance once responding starts. After a reinforcer is delivered, however, a *postreinforcement pause* usually occurs, after which responding begins again. This pause after the delivery of a reinforcer makes FR schedules somewhat inefficient. Piecework is an example of FR responding. For example, an apple picker works rapidly once he begins picking apples, but he pauses after the box is full. Then he picks rapidly until the next box is filled, and so on.

> **KEY TERM:** *Fixed-Ratio (FR) Schedule*
> An FR schedule is a reinforcement schedule whereby a reinforcer is delivered only after a fixed number of responses have been completed.

Variable-Ratio Schedules. In a *variable-ratio (VR) schedule,* the number of responses that must be emitted before a reinforcer is delivered varies. The number corresponding with the VR schedule indicates the average number of responses that must occur before a reinforcer is delivered. For example, on a VR 10 schedule, a reinforcer may be delivered after the 2nd, 14th, 7th, 9th, and 18th responses. (Note that the average of these numbers is 10.) The key aspect of these schedules is that reinforcer delivery is somewhat unpredictable. This unpredictability in reinforcer delivery tends to produce high, steady rates of performance and is usually not characterized by the post reinforcement pauses associated with FR schedules. For this reason, VR schedules work well in classrooms, homes, and businesses. Examples of VR schedules include fields of sales where a variable number of attempts are reinforced and blind dates, which are said to be on a large VR schedule.

KEY TERM: *Variable-Ratio (VR) Schedule*

A VR schedule is a semirandom reinforcement schedule whereby a reinforcer is delivered only after an average number of responses has been completed. The number of required responses varies from the delivery of one reinforcer to the next.

Fixed-Interval Schedules. With interval schedules, the first behavior to be emitted after a certain amount of time passes is reinforced. *Fixed-interval (FI) schedules* specify the exact amount of time that must pass before a behavior is reinforced. An FI 7 schedule means that the first target response that occurs after exactly 7 minutes is reinforced. The reinforcer is not delivered until the interval expires and the person responds. The pattern of responding that emerges from an FI schedule consists of very little responding at the beginning of an interval, followed by a burst of activity at the end of the interval. The behavior of members of Congress is on an FI schedule: Few bills are passed at the beginning of a session, and many are passed at the end of a session, when re-election is looming. Fixed-interval schedules are inefficient schedules of reinforcement, but unfortunately they are the schedule most often used in schools. For example, reinforcers (e.g., grades, praise) are generally not available until after the due date for a given assignment. Therefore, students typically engage in very low rates of responding when an assignment is first given because they know reinforcement will not occur for some time. It is only when the due date draws near, and reinforcers are available, that students begin to work.

KEY TERM: *Fixed-Interval (FI) Schedule*

An FI schedule is a reinforcement schedule whereby a reinforcer is delivered for the first response that occurs after a fixed amount of time has elapsed.

Variable-Interval Schedules. A *variable-interval (VI) schedule* specifies the average amount of time that must pass before a behavior is reinforced. The actual amount of time varies from one response to the next. On a VI 7 schedule, the first target response that occurs after 3, 12, 9, 2, 5, and 11 minutes is reinforced. (Note that the average of these numbers is 7.) Variable-interval schedules produce steady and moderate rates of response. The response rate is higher than that generated by FI schedules, but not as high as FR and VR schedules. The game of musical chairs is on a VI schedule, and the participants maintain a steady rate of alertness. Pop quizzes, another example of VI schedules, keep students studying at a steady but not frantic rate.

KEY TERM: *Variable-Interval (VI) Schedule*
A VI schedule is a semirandom reinforcement schedule whereby a reinforcer is delivered for the first response that occurs after an average amount of time has elapsed.

The following facts may help people remember which schedules produce which effects:

Ratio schedules = high rates

Interval schedules = low rates

Fixed schedules = pauses

Variable schedules = steady responding

These facts can be combined to reveal that FI schedules produce low rates of response with pauses, VR schedules produce steady and high rates, and so on. One final key point about reinforcement schedules is that continuous schedules do not occur very often in the real world. As stated earlier, CRF schedules work well for teaching a new behavior. However, for the behavior to become more persistent and last over time, use an intermittent schedule (preferably a VR or VI) and reinforcers that can be found in the person's natural environment.

Basic Principles Quiz 4

1. Why would it be best to use a CRF schedule when reinforcing a new behavior?

---

2. Why do ratio schedules, rather than interval schedules, produce higher rates of response?

_____

_____

_____

_____

_____

3. Once a behavior is established, what kind of reinforcement schedule should be used to maintain the behavior? Why?

_____

_____

_____

_____

_____

4. Give an example of how reinforcement might be arranged on a VR 15 schedule.

_____

_____

_____

_____

_____

RESPONDING IN THE PRESENCE OF SPECIFIC STIMULI

Events That Precede Behavior

Antecedents of Behavior

So far we have emphasized the manner in which events that follow a behavior affect the future rate of that behavior. Events that precede a behavior also affect its occurrence. These events are called *antecedent stimuli* and also have a major effect on behavior. For example, parents call their children in for dinner, and the children immediately come into the kitchen. The school bell rings, and students immediately grab their belongings and line up for dismissal. Bosses ask secretaries to proofread their work, and many do as they are requested. Antecedents are important because they set the occasion for behavior to occur. In these examples, behavior did not occur (e.g., coming into the kitchen, lining up for dismissal, or proofreading work) until some stimulus in the environment signaled the appropriate behavior. Looking at these signals, or antecedents, as well as the consequences that follow the behavior is often referred to as the *ABCs of behavior* (see Figure 6).

> **KEY TERM:** *Antecedents*
> Antecedents are events that occur prior to behavior and can influence the rate of occurrence of the behavior.

A = Antecedent
B = Behavior
C = Consequences

Figure 6. The ABCs of behavior.

Stimulus Control

Most antecedent events have no natural power to produce behavior. These initially neutral stimuli, however, can come to have major effects on behavior because of the way they are paired with consequences. Some stimuli act as cues to emit certain behaviors. These cues are called *discriminative stimuli* (S^D). They inform us that, if we make certain responses in their presence, reinforcement is likely to follow. Other stimuli, which do not signal reinforcement for a behavior, are called *nondiscriminative stimuli,* or *S-deltas* (S^Δ). They tell us not to emit those responses in their presence.

The process of teaching someone to make a discrimination between an S^D and an S^Δ is called *differential reinforcement*. This means that people consistently reinforce a behavior in the presence of a certain S^D. People never reinforce it in the presence of other stimuli (S^Δ). Soon it is apparent that the behavior is emitted only in the presence of the S^D and not the S^Δ.

| S^D | Response | Reinforcement | S^D | Response | Reinforcement |
| S^Δ | Response | No Reinforcement | S^Δ | No Response | |

When a behavior reliably occurs in the presence of one stimulus but does not occur in its absence, the behavior is said to be under *stimulus control.* We see examples of stimulus control in many environments. Take the situation in which the teacher presents a math problem and the student gives the answer. Correct answers are reinforced, and incorrect answers are not reinforced. Stimulus control is demonstrated when the student reliably gives the correct answer (e.g., 7) in the presence of the problem (e.g., 3 + 4 = _____). In the examples already discussed, walking to the dinner table, gathering belongings, and proofreading work are behaviors under stimulus control. These behaviors only occur in the presence of specific environmental stimuli. At times, the degree of stimulus control is remarkable, such as when a motorist sits at a red light at 3 A.M. with no other cars or police officers in sight.

To provide an optimal learning environment, employers, parents, and teachers must provide clear S^Ds and S^Δs so that others are able to discriminate conditions that lead to reinforcement from those conditions that do not. For example, classroom rules that explicitly state expectations help students identify behaviors that result in reinforcement.

KEY TERM: *Stimulus Control*

Stimulus control involves emitting a behavior reliably under specific stimulus conditions.

Antecedents That Trigger Inappropriate Behavior

The process by which stimulus control is developed can result in both appropriate and inappropriate behavior. In the example just discussed, the teacher differentially reinforced the correct answer to the math problem. The appropriate response (i.e., writing the number 7) to the stimulus (i.e., 3 + 4 = _____) is certainly an example of stimulus control. However, stimulus control can result in a less than appropriate behavior. For example, Mr. L notes that Sam is a model student except when she is around Rachel. At such times, Sam often makes inappropriate comments and Rachel laughs, which seems to add fuel to the fire. In this example, Rachel's presence serves as an S^D to signal that the behavior of stating inappropriate comments will be reinforced (i.e., attention and laughter). However, when Sam sits next to Ben, no such behavior is observed, probably because Ben pays no attention to Sam. In this case, Ben serves as an S^Δ, which signals that a reinforcer for inappropriate comments is not available.

Sometimes certain antecedents are said to trigger problem behavior. These triggers are S^Ds that signal the availability of reinforcers for the behavior. For example, Lorraine calls Sue a rude name during recess. Lorraine retaliates by hitting Sue, who then promptly runs to the other side of the playground. In this example, Sue's name-calling served as an S^D (i.e., trigger) to signal that hitting behavior would be reinforced (i.e., Sue leaving Lorraine alone). In such cases, where antecedent events trigger problem behavior, practitioners can modify or remove the antecedents to affect changes in behavior.

Basic Principles Quiz 5

1. Describe the ABCs model of behavior. Give three examples of how this model may operate at home.

_____

_____

_____

_____

2. What is *stimulus control*? Give an example from your own life of one behavior that is under stimulus control and one that is not.

_____

_____

_____

_____

3. What is the difference between an S^D and an S^Δ?

_____

_____

_____

_____

_____

4. Describe how an antecedent stimulus can serve as an S^D and "trigger" inappropriate behavior.

_____

_____

_____

_____

_____

USING REINFORCEMENT TO INCREASE KNOWN BEHAVIORS

One powerful use of reinforcement is to increase the occurrence of behavior already in the learner's repertoire. Perhaps the first step in this process is to determine possible reinforcing consequences for the desired behavior. In this section, we discuss several different types of reinforcers as well as several methods to identify appropriate reinforcers for use in applied settings.

Types of Positive Reinforcers

There are four different classifications of positive reinforcers: tangible, social, activity, and token. The following sections discuss each of these classifications in detail.

Tangible Reinforcers

Consumable and other types of tangible reinforcers, such as candy, trinkets, and toys, can be powerful motivators for human behavior. Also, with populations such as people with severe cognitive impairments, a reinforcer such as food might be the only effective reinforcer available. However, in most cases practitioners should look for alternatives because tangible reinforcers are often expensive and because many people find it socially unacceptable to use reinforcers such as candy for high school students or adult employees. Alternatives such as activity, social, and token reinforcers are both powerful and socially acceptable.

> **KEY TERM:** *Tangible Reinforcers*
> Tangible reinforcers are consumables and small objects and may include items such as food, toys, magazines, comic books, coloring books, clothes, and appliances.

Activity Reinforcers

Favorite activities undoubtedly constitute a powerful type of reinforcer. Also, many appealing activity reinforcers are free or inexpensive. Effective activity reinforcers in the schools include free time, helping the secretary or custodian, lining up first, being a messenger, and handing out papers. Activity reinforcers in the home include being allowed to stay up late, going out for a pizza or to a movie, and having a friend sleep over. Activity reinforcers in the workplace include parking in a preferred spot and receiving favored job assignments.

We highly recommend the use of activity reinforcers. However, such use can pose problems. First, some activities such as free time in a school might result in disorderly play and might be disruptive to other classes. Also, it is not always possible to provide activity reinforcers in a timely manner, resulting in a delay of reinforcement. Finally, some activity reinforcers such as attending a sports event on a certain date must be provided on an all-or-none basis, limiting flexible application of those reinforcers.

> **KEY TERM:** *Activity Reinforcers*
>
> Activity reinforcers are preferred events and may include privileges such as having free time, having extra computer time, receiving a day off from work, attending a movie, listening to a CD, or being the classroom messenger.

Social Reinforcement

No form of reinforcement is less expensive, easier to deliver, and probably more underused than social reinforcement. Examples of social reinforcers include compliments, handshakes, smiles, high fives, words of appreciation, letters of commendation, honor rolls, and award certificates.

> **KEY TERM:** *Social Reinforcers*
>
> Social reinforcers are events or objects that are valued by the community and may include Employee-of-the-Month designations, letters of congratulation, handshakes, pats on the back, attention, praise, and notes home from teachers.

Token Reinforcers

A *token reinforcer* is a generalized reinforcer that is useful in a variety of environments. A token can be a symbol such as a check mark or a smiley face, or it can be a tangible item such as a trading stamp, a poker chip, a ticket, or a star. In most cases, awarding a token alone will not affect behavior. Tokens, however, can be quite powerful when they are exchangeable for a variety of other items or activities, known as *back-up reinforcers*. Tokens are similar to money in that they can be exchanged for tickets to shows, gift certificates, field trips, and special privileges. Parents use a token reinforcement procedure when they put stars on a calendar for appropriate behavior and allow their children to exchange them for a favored item. Teachers use token systems when they rate a student's behavior on a scale of 1 to 10 four times each day and then allow that student to exchange the points for extra computer time. Companies use token systems when they award salespeople free trips for successfully completing a specified number of sales.

Token reinforcement systems are effective for a variety of reasons:

1. Awarding tokens in a classroom does not disrupt the environment, unlike the immediate awarding of activity reinforcers. In fact, tokens can be used to purchase activity reinforcers at a later time. This helps bridge the gap between an appropriate behavior and the delivery of an activity reinforcer.

2. Because tokens are associated with many back-up reinforcers, they do not depend on any one condition of deprivation, which might be the case with a single food reinforcer.

3. Unlike some other reinforcers, tokens can be delivered immediately after an appropriate behavior occurs.

4. Because tokens are tangible and can be seen by the recipient, they provide continuous feedback to the learner.

5. Tokens can be broken into small segments and, therefore, allow for graded reinforcement. For example, 25 tokens can be exchanged for 1 day without having to do household chores, whereas 50 tokens can be exchanged for 2 days.

6. Tokens can be exchanged for unusual or expensive reinforcers. A child, for example, could save his or her tokens over several weeks for a trip to an amusement park.

7. Tokens help teachers, parents, and employers set clear goals. For example, teachers can indicate the number of tokens that can be earned for turning in assignments on time, lining up quietly, and transitioning between classes efficiently. Goals can be set to try to beat the scores from the previous week.

8. There is no maximum number of tokens a person can earn.

9. Token systems help people learn to delay gratification while still providing immediate feedback.

10. Token systems can be used with one individual, several individuals, or an entire group.

11. Token systems are typically more powerful than other reinforcement systems because they are delivered immediately and result in a reinforcer that is selected by the individual.

Before someone sets up a token reinforcement system, certain elements must be in place. First, the desired behaviors need to be specified. Second, the items that can be exchanged for tokens (i.e., the back-up reinforcers) must be clear. Third, a clear relationship must exist between the desired behaviors, the tokens, and the back-up reinforcers. For example, getting 20 problems correct can be worth 5 tokens, which are exchangeable for a short break; or receiving the Employee of the Month award 3 times can be exchanged for 1 extra week of vacation. Finally, the time at which the back-up reinforcers may be purchased must be clear.

Sometimes it is necessary to use tokens and tangible reinforcers to condition naturally available reinforcers. Children, who have never responded to natural reinforcers such as adult approval or pride in a job well done, will work hard for tokens that allow them to have things they want or to do things they want to do. It is very important to pair the tokens with adult approval and praise. This pairing procedure allows for the gradual withdrawal of the tokens so that more natural reinforcers (e.g., verbal praise) take over.

As already indicated, tokens are extremely effective in changing behavior. However, people rarely use tokens. One problem might be the expense of the programs. More likely, the problem is the complexity of many systems. Therefore, we recommend that people who use token systems keep them as simple as possible. Start out delivering tokens for just a few behaviors, and then add more target behaviors over time. Make the record-keeping system as simple and as student-centered as possible. Use inexpensive back-up reinforcers at first, only adding more expensive items as needed to maintain behavior. The bottom line is that simple systems that get used are always more effective than more elaborate systems that are discontinued after several days because they are too cumbersome to implement.

> **KEY TERM:** *Token Reinforcer*
> A token reinforcer is a neutral stimulus that can be exchanged
> for something of value at a later time. Examples of token
> reinforcers include symbols such as check marks, smiley faces,
> or gift certificates.

Basic Principles Quiz 6

1. Describe a behavior problem you are presently encounter-
   ing. Devise a program to deal with the problem that makes
   use of tangible, activity, social, and token reinforcers.

   _____

   _____

   _____

   _____

   _____

   _____

2. Suppose the expression "Well done" is not a social reinforcer
   for someone. Indicate how you could make the expression
   into a social reinforcer.

   _____

   _____

   _____

   _____

   _____

   _____

3. Why is a gift certificate a less appealing reinforcer than money?

_____

_____

_____

_____

4. Describe a token reinforcement system that would be relatively easy to implement.

_____

_____

_____

_____

5. Schools are already using a token reinforcement system: student grades. Why is this token system so often ineffective?

_____

_____

_____

_____

6. Compare the advantages and disadvantages of token systems versus other reinforcement systems.

_____

_____

_____

_____

_____

Selecting Appropriate Reinforcers

An important factor in a successful behavioral program is selecting an effective reinforcer. This selection can be achieved in several ways. One of the simplest ways is to note what follows a behavior. The behavior of a preschool child who is consistently comforted after crying is probably reinforced by adult attention. An adult with developmental disabilities who consistently leaves the group home to go to a fast food restaurant is likely to work for the opportunity to go to the restaurant.

There are also systematic ways to identify appropriate reinforcers. For example, a teacher, parent, or employer could ask people to identify effective reinforcers for their behavior. Admittedly, when people are asked to do this, they might request reinforcers that are prohibitively expensive or difficult to procure. However, by persevering in the process, it is possible to pinpoint effective and reasonable reinforcers. A second way to systematically identify potential reinforcers is to give the person a list of reinforcers and have him or her select from items and events on the list. This method provides an effective way to limit reinforcers that may be difficult to provide. When this is done, several potential reinforcers should be selected to allow for variety. Another way to identify a potential reinforcer is to note what a person spends a lot of time doing. If someone spends a great deal of time in an activity, that activity is likely to be a reinforcer. Such events then can be made contingent on behavior and are likely to reinforce desired behaviors. For example, if a child spends a great deal of time watching television, this activity can be provided contingent on behaviors such as completing chores. If a student is found reading a magazine in English class, he or she can be awarded magazine reading time for completing English assignments. Finally, a potential reinforcer may be ineffective because a person has never experienced it. In such cases one can use a *reinforcer sampling* procedure in which a person engages in the reinforcing event for a short time before being required to earn it. Car salespeople take advantage of this process when they have potential customers sample a new car over the weekend. If a teacher wants to use a game such as Seven Up as a reinforcer and the students are not familiar with the game, the teacher can have the children play the game for 5 minutes before they are required to work for it.

Several factors characterize a well-selected reinforcer. One factor is that the reinforcer is a naturally occurring consequence. That is, the reinforcer is one that is commonly present in a person's environment. Such reinforcers are often less costly and easier to arrange than contrived reinforcers. Therefore, praise is a more natural reinforcer than posting a list of outstanding students, and a bonus in a paycheck is easier to provide than a trip to an exotic island.

Natural reinforcers are more likely to continue to be available after the behavior has been established. If the reinforcers are natural to the situation, the person receiving them is more likely to come in contact with them in the natural environment after the systematic reinforcement program ends. Moving reinforcers from contrived to natural is very important if a target behavior is to continue to occur after the formal behavior change program has been withdrawn. Thus, a boy who receives time to engage in leisure reading activities for completing math assignments is more likely to continue to receive this reinforcer when he passes on to the next grade than he would if the original reinforcer had been candy or a toy.

People should always strive to bring the persons with whom they work in contact with natural reinforcers to maintain the behavior and attempt to arrange or rearrange the reinforcers occurring naturally in the environment to their advantage. If reinforcers have been presented in the past on a noncontingent basis, they may have gone to waste. Even worse, the person of concern has developed patterns of behavior that will make him or her less likely to come in contact with all the reinforcers, which would otherwise be available.

One mother was concerned about her 4-year-old son, who took more than 2 hours to dress himself in the morning. He preferred to watch television and would not dress quickly unless she scolded him severely, spanked him, or dressed him herself. She instituted a program in which watching television was contingent on getting dressed within 10 minutes of getting out of bed each morning. As a result, her son came into contact with a number of reinforcers that had not been available before. He still got to see his favorite television programs, and he received praise from his mother and father for his behavior. Nagging, spanking, and other unpleasant actions were avoided. In addition, the son's opinion of himself changed. He told his grandmother that he was no longer a baby because he got up and got dressed on time by himself.

Another characteristic of a reinforcer that will enhance its effectiveness is novelty. People can be very motivated to work for a surprise. The surprise reinforcer can be intermingled with a predictable but desirable reinforcer. Therefore, it is important to become skilled at selecting new and different reinforcers to maintain high behavior rates. For example, in addition to delivering reinforcers that are typically available to her students, a teacher may occasionally give students raffle tickets for appropriate behavior. That teacher then can hold a drawing for novel prizes at random times throughout the week.

The potential reinforcers listed in Table 1 are consequent events that have been used successfully to increase the strength of behaviors of these varying populations. They may include reinforcers that can be used in the home, in school, or in working environments.

(text continues on p. 55)

TABLE I
Sample Reinforcers

Potential Reinforcers for Ages 0–4 at Home

Infant

Bright shiny objects

Rocking to sleep

Humming or singing

Moving or waving toy
   above crib

Change of diaper

Soft fuzzy toys

Smelling flower

Cooing

Finger paint

Blanket

Tasting cake batter,
   soda, etc.

Riding in a stroller

Being tossed in air

Taking a bath

Tangible Toys

Snacks

Dessert

New shoes

Favorite food

Candy and other sweets

Drink of water, juice, etc.

Ice cream from truck

Activities

Trip to park

Playing with friends

Getting in bed with
   parents

Making mud pies

Bedtime story

Playing on swing set

Spending the night
   with friends or
   grandparents

Being lifted into air

Opportunity to feed pet

Rocking

Games

Making noises (rattles,
   bells)

Swinging on foot (horsey
   ride)

Finger play

Eating out

Rocking in rocking chair

Wearing parent's
   clothing

Playing with clay

Going someplace alone
   with Dad

Helping plan day's
   activities

Helping Mom or Dad

Longer time in bathtub

Riding on bicycle with
   Mom

Whirling in circle by
   arms

Special hour, day

Watching lightning

Playing in sandbox

Popping balloon

Bouncing on bed

Playing outside

Riding tricycle

Staying up late

Trip to zoo

Piggyback ride

Bubble bath

Singing song

Sitting on lap

Whirling in chair

Flushing the toilet

Riding on Dad's
   shoulders

Going outside at night

Family night

Helping hold baby

Swimming

(continues)

TABLE I. *Continued.*
Sample Reinforcers

Activities *(continued)*

Taking a picture of how good child is	Sitting in chair with parent	Being pulled in wagon
Playing with magnet	Not having to take bath one night	Carrying purse or briefcase
Talking into tape recorder	Blowing bubbles	
	Blowing out match	

Social

Physical contact, hugs, kisses, tickles	Verbal praise	Smiling
Stroking under chin	Winks	Indirect praise, telling someone else how good he or she is
Talking to child	Eye contact	

Tokens

Money	Stars on chart

Potential Reinforcers for Ages 5–11 at Home

Tangible

Toys	Snacks	Clothing
Pets	Own bedroom	Jigsaw puzzles
Books		

Activities

Dressing up in adult clothes	Freedom from chores	Going alone on a trip by bus, plane, etc.
Trip to park	Holding hand while walking	Holding nails while Dad hammers
Playing with friends	Using telephone	Playing favorite tapes and CDs
Camping in backyard	Wearing parent's clothes	Coloring in coloring book
Bedtime story	Setting the table	Riding next to window in car
Playing on swing set	Opening coffee can, smelling aroma	Choosing menu for meal
Spending night with friends or grandparents	Decorating home for holidays	
Going to a ball game		
Eating out		

(continues)

TABLE I. *Continued.*
Sample Reinforcers

Activities (continued)

Going someplace alone with Dad

Baking something in kitchen

Planning a day's activities

Riding on bicycle

Fishing trip with Mom

Choice of television program

Playing with magnifying glass

Helping make dessert, popcorn, etc.

Helping take a gift to a friend

"Sit" for younger children while Mom is near

Feeding the baby

Late bedtime

Going to movies (especially with a friend)

Calling Grandma to tell of successes

Riding escalator three or four times at the store

Displaying schoolwork on refrigerator door

Letting child buy something

Planting a garden

Playing with magnet

Social

Handshake

Verbal praise

Telling grandparents of accomplishments

Hugs

Kisses

Tokens

Money

Own bank account

Stars on chart

Increase in allowance

Potential Reinforcers for Ages 12–18 at Home

Tangible

Favorite meal

Clothes

Books

Radio

Bicycle

Electric razor, hairbrush, hair dryer

Having own room

Having a soda

Television

Watch

Selecting own gift

Makeup

Private phone

Stereo

Jewelry

Guitar

CDs

Activities

Dating privileges

Participating in activities with friends

Dating during week

Sewing own clothes

Watching television (choose program)

Part-time job

Taking car to school for a day

Getting driver's license

(continues)

TABLE I. *Continued.*
Sample Reinforcers

Activities (continued)

Having friends over
Dance or music lessons
Refrigerator privileges
Redecorating own room
Extended curfew
Car privileges
Staying up late
Staying overnight with
   friends
Time off from chores
Kidding and joking
Choosing own bedtime

Camping out
Summer camp
Expensive haircut
Going to Disneyland
   with parents
Skating
Additional time on
   telephone
Playing stereo
Making trip alone on bus
   or plane

Reading
Opportunity to earn
   money
Selection of television
   program
Chairing family meeting
Getting to use family
   camera
Going to amusement
   park
Discussion with parents
Allowed to sit alone
   when family eats out
Getting to sleep late on
   weekend

Social

Smiles
Attention when talking
"OK" gesture with
   thumb and finger

Being asked for opinion
Hugs

Verbal praise
Head nods
Winks

Tokens

Extra money
Having own checking
   account

Allowance
Driver's license

Magazine subscription
Gift certificate

Potential Reinforcers for Elementary School Students

Tangible

Food

Activities

Recess (extra or longer)
Group leader
Going to library
Room "manager"

Crafts activities
Head of lunch line
Erasing boards

Performing before a
   group
Helping custodian
Fixing bulletin board

(continues)

TABLE I. *Continued.*

Sample Reinforcers

Activities *(continued)*

Hall monitor

Listening to records

Choosing song in music class

Individual conference on progress

Field trips

Sharpening pencil

Reading own composition to class

No homework

Choice of seat mate (for day, week, permanent)

Raise flag for day or week

Watch self on videotape

Passing out milk

Having parents visit

Making gift for parent

Riding in seat behind bus driver

Playing instruments

Extra computer time

Going to principal's office

After-school activity

Tutoring another pupil

Day to chew gum in class

Having picture taken

Leading class in singing

Picnics

Cafeteria helper

Displaying work to another class

Demonstrating hobby to class

Host in front hallway on parents' day

Going home early

Planning daily schedule

Collecting lunch tickets

Independent study

Principal's helper for day

Free activity in corner of room (puzzles, games)

Scheduling group, then individual activities

Running errands

First or last in line

Early dismissal

Playing game

Helping librarian

Viewing films

Party

Drink of water

Student government activity

Displaying work to principal

Making and viewing videotape

Team captain

Selecting bulletin board topic

Academic contests

Story time

Having lunch with teacher or principal

Scheduling quiet, then noisy activities

Time to lie on floor, sit on desk, study outside

Social

Smiles, winks

Verbal praise

Posting picture (student of month)

Being voted most improved student in academic area

Eye contact

Displaying picture of self

Getting to time self with stopwatch

(continues)

TABLE I. *Continued.*

Sample Reinforcers

Social *(continued)*

Principal praise	Phone call to parents	Homework (good papers) on bulletin board
Pat on back	Positive comments written on papers	Being on school patrol

Tokens

Badges to be worn for day, signifying staff to give positive attention	Seeing progress toward going on picnic on graph	Honor roll
Grades	Points	Noting academic progress
Stars	Happy face on paper	Special certificate of completed work
	Big red "A" on paper	

Potential Reinforcers for Secondary School Students

Tangible

Posters	Blank tapes	Pizza, dried fruit
Sports equipment	Paperback books	Nuts, pretzels, chips
Music tapes	Ticket to show	Juice, soft drinks
Magazines	Demo CDs	

Activities

Having extra free time	Going on a field trip	Watching a DVD
Playing checkers, chess, or card game	Having extra gym time	Having a class outside
Listening to private radio or CD	Having extra lunch time	Observing a science demonstration
Having classroom party	Working on computer	Talking to another student
	Teaching another student	Playing cards
	Having day with no homework	

Social

Smiles, winks, handshakes	Complimentary phone call to student or parents	Honor roll
Thumbs up		Complimentary note
Pat on back	High achievement list	Private compliment

(continues)

TABLE I. *Continued.*
Sample Reinforcers

Tokens

Increasing test grade
Increasing course grade
Gift certificate

Point card with back-up
    reinforcers

Noting academic
    progress on chart

Potential Reinforcers on the Job

Tangible

Prizes, television sets,
    stereos, carpeting,
    etc.
Small gifts (flowers for
    secretary)
Something to decorate
    office or work area
Special parking space

Car allowance
Free coffee
Free lunch
Water cooler
More comfortable chair
Special place to store
    personal belongings

Convert room for
    lounge
Personal mailbox
Larger office
Paid lunch allowance
Thermostat in office
Quiet area for break
Business card

Activities

Time off
Longer coffee breaks
Assisting someone with
    job
Trips (Hawaii, Bahamas)
Trips to conventions,
    workshops
Extra help on job
Transfer request
    accepted
Tenure or other
    evidence of job
    security
Not having to "punch"
    clock
Leaving 5 minutes early
Lunch paid for by the
    boss

Choice of shift
Choice of location for
    work station
Reduced work load
Promotion to better job
Having lunch, vacation
    with boss
Added responsibilities
Extra vacation
Personal business time
    off
Supervising trainee
Invitation to participate
    in special project
Surfing the Internet

Access to secretarial
    help
Piped-in music
Parties, social events
Day off for birthday
Coming in late for having
    worked extra hours
Private office
Being able to take
    spouse to convention,
    or not being required
    to take spouse to
    convention
Paid for continuing
    education
Voice in decision making

(continues)

TABLE I. *Continued.*

Sample Reinforcers

Social

Verbal praise from supervisor	Picture or name in company paper	Greeting from boss
Group recognition for achievement	Listening to suggestions	Asking person to explain her or his work to visitors
Eye contact	Posting production charts	Recognition for suggestions
Employee of week, month, year	Praise from peers	Special job title
New title	Good work evaluation	Note of appreciation
	Name on desk or office door	

Tokens

Merit salary increase	Bonus	Free tickets to recreation or social event
Certificate of outstanding performance	Points backed by prizes	Telephone credit card

Potential Reinforcers for Spouses or Significant Others

Tangible

Clothes	Jewelry	Furniture
Flowers	Special cards	Car
Making breakfast in bed	Magazine subscription	Perfume/cologne

Activities

Going out to eat	Going grocery shopping together	Weekend away from kids
Telephone call during day	Having hair brushed	Sleeping late on weekends
Going dancing	Babysitting	Time alone
Time to talk	Massage	Consulting about important decisions
Time off from household responsibilities	Remembering important occasions	Chance to select movie
Night out alone	Choosing side of bed to sleep on	Attention in public
Being warned when in-laws are coming		Surprise party

(continues)

TABLE I. *Continued.*
Sample Reinforcers

Social

Compliments in presence of another person	Compliments on appearance	Eye contact
Verbal praise, compliments	Pet name	Saying, "I love you"
Smiles	Positive feedback on household jobs	Romantic dialogue
Listening intently	Back rubs, hugs, kisses, and other physical contact	No mention of past mistakes
Being on time for dinner		Phone call

Tokens

Extra money	Memberships	Gift certificate

▶ **Assignment:** Describe three different ways to identify a reinforcer for the following people:

1. A child _____

_____

2. An adult _____

_____

3. Yourself _____

_____

Basic Principles Quiz 7

Fred was a 17-year-old junior in high school. He frequently skipped classes and was receiving Ds and Fs in all his classes except for gym. He was also argumentative at home. He frequently shouted at his parents and claimed that they did not give him enough allowance or access to the car, even though his parents owned two cars. He also objected because his mother nagged him about how he was doing in school, keeping his room clean, and coming in on time. The school counselor tried setting up a program whereby Fred could earn privileges, such as going to assemblies or visiting the student lounge, for going to class or getting good grades. However, Fred did not respond to the program but instead continued to skip classes other than gym. He frequently disappeared to play video games at a shopping mall or basketball at an outdoor court in a nearby playground.

1. Why did the school counselor's program fail?

   _____

   _____

   _____

   _____

   _____

2. Fred's program suggests that certain activities might be reinforcers for him. What are those activities?

   _____

   _____

   _____

   _____

3. Select one of Fred's behaviors and suggest a contingency you think might be effective in changing the behavior.

   _____

   _____

   _____

   _____

   _____

4. Suggest a reinforcer sampling procedure the parents might use to increase the probability that Fred will respond to a reinforcer they might offer.

_____

_____

_____

_____

_____

_____

_____

Using Verbal Praise

The most common form of social reinforcement is praise. Praise can be delivered immediately after a behavior occurs, it costs nothing, it is not disruptive to the surrounding environment, and it requires no preparation for its delivery. Examples of praise include such comments as, "Thanks for getting the job done so quickly," "You are really paying attention today," and "I really like the way you helped him with his geometry lesson." The following is a list of guidelines on the use of praise:

1. Make praise contingent on appropriate behavior. If praise is used indiscriminately, it will reinforce both inappropriate and appropriate behaviors.

2. Praise should sound and be sincere. Sincerity can be achieved by making eye contact with the person and varying the compliments. Instead of saying "Very good!" over and over, try saying "Fantastic!" or "Cool!" or other terms in vogue at the moment. Also, vary the expression and

inflection in your voice to show different amounts of enthusiasm.

3. When giving social reinforcers, smile, make eye contact, and ask questions about what the other person says. Few things are more reinforcing. On the other hand, persons who merely wait to jump in and say what they want to say are very offensive.

4. Pair social reinforcement with other reinforcers by lending a helping hand or giving other reinforcers with a smile and a word of praise.

5. Become skilled at private, indirect, and public praise. You can provide private praise with a handshake, a quiet word, a written note, or a drawing of a happy face. From a distance, private praise is possible through a smile, a gesture, a silently mouthed word, a nod of the head, or a thumbs-up. People who become skilled at emitting such behaviors are people others tend to like and are more likely to inspire similar positive responses.

6. Another important skill is the use of social reinforcement in conjunction with other available reinforcers. Frequent praise or shows of approval while providing other reinforcers can result in the following positive outcomes:

   a. The person with whom you are working will be more likely to find the praise and positive attention of others reinforcing. That is sometimes the only reinforcer available.

   b. Your presence may become reinforcing to the person, and your attention and interest will be more effective in other situations.

   c. Because others learn a great deal through imitation, the persons with whom you come in contact will much more likely learn to reinforce other people's behavior with attention. This is one of the most important skills anyone can learn.

7. Be specific in your praise. Research has shown that specific praise is usually more effective than general praise. Thus, a teacher will be a more effective reinforcing agent if she tells Herb, "That's such good work! You worked five out of six problems correctly," than if she says, "It looks like you're working better, Herb. I'm proud of you." Being specific helps clarify what behavior resulted in the praise. In this case, correct answers rather than sitting quietly and not disturbing neighbors produced praise. In the same way, the boss's statement "Chris, I really appreciate how you stayed late and typed up that report without errors. It helped me make that sale" will likely be more effective than "Chris, you're a good secretary. Thanks for all you do."

In spite of almost universal agreement that people should use praise regularly, it is a seldom used procedure. Parents might go days without complimenting their well-behaved children. Teachers might use praise once an hour when they could be using it once a minute. Employers might go years without putting a complimentary note in an employee's mailbox. If social reinforcement is such a good procedure, why do so few people use it? One possibility is that some people feel insincere when praising others. This problem is likely to be alleviated when you continually use praise and when such praise encounters a pleasant reaction and improved behavior from the recipient. A more likely problem is that appropriate behavior does not call attention to itself. In other words, it is a "squeaky wheel" problem. There are at least two ways to overcome this difficulty. One is to have a timer go off at different intervals. At those times, for example, a teacher or a factory supervisor checks to see who is working appropriately and praises those who are. A second way is to keep track of the number of times you use praise each day and to try to increase the daily total.

▶ **Assignment:** For 2 or 3 days next week, keep track of the rate at which you deliver social praise to an individual or group. Then try to increase the rate by 3, 5, or even 10 or more times. Report the results.

_____

_____

_____

_____

Contingency Contracting

In some situations a person such as a parent, teacher, or employer embarks on a program to change the behavior of a child, student, or employee. Although most human interactions proceed naturally in this way, some people object to the arrangement because they see it as coercive and controlling. Some people believe that all parties should first agree to a behavior-change program before it proceeds. Such people might also suggest that if a person buys into the program he or she is more likely to participate and to show behavioral gains. One manner of achieving these ends is through a contingency contract. A *contingency contract* is a written agreement between at least two parties that specifies the type and quantity of reinforcers one party will deliver if the other party meets specified goals. The agreement can be between an employer and employee or between a teacher, a parent, and a student, or it may take other forms. Some contracts also specify bonuses for outstanding performance and penalties for inappropriate behaviors. The explicit, written form of a contract makes contingencies clear and helps all parties meet their responsibilities. As the word *contract* implies, the terms of the agreement should involve negotiation between all parties and should specify an expiration date or the terms under which the contract can be renegotiated (e.g., one party is unhappy with it). Figure 7 shows an example of a contract between a 9-year-old boy and his mother.

Writing effective contracts involves following several guidelines. First, contracts should specify the positive rather than the negative. That is, contracts should emphasize what a person can achieve for meeting the terms of the contract, rather than penalties for not meeting behavioral criteria. The contract should provide small reinforcers for reasonable improvement, rather than large rewards for unrealistic gains. Contracts should also provide for short-term rather than long-term reinforcers. Also, the terms of the contract should be clear to all parties. Finally, as progress occurs, additional contracts may be written over time, increasing the criteria for rewards to help fade out the formal program.

KEY TERM: *Contingency Contract*

A contingency contract is a document between two parties that specifies the contingencies for the delivery of reinforcers. Contingency contracts are usually written as if–then statements (e.g., If Sydney cleans her room, then Mom will take her to the mall).

Contract

We agree that whenever Hector puts away his toys at the end of the day and takes out the trash when requested, he will receive 1 point. When he receives 5 points on his point card, he will be allowed to have a friend sleep over on the weekend or go to a movie of his choosing.

3/3/05	Hector Toro	Juanita Toro
Expiration Date	Hector's Signature	Parent's Signature

Points Accumulated

1	2	3	4	5
X	X			

Figure 7. Contingency contract sample.

▶ **Assignment:** Suggest a contingency contract for one of the following:

1. Between a parent and teenager who stays out past curfew

2. Among a teacher, a parent, and a student who fails to complete homework

3. Between domestic partners who do not pick up their belongings

_____

_____

_____

High-*p* Request Sequences

Another reinforcement-based technique that can be used to increase appropriate behavior is *high-probability request sequences.* In this intervention, a series of requests or tasks with a high probability of compliance (high-*p*) is delivered prior to a request with a low probability of compliance (low-*p*). The response momentum that is created by compliance and subsequent reinforcement of high-*p* behaviors often carries over and results in compliance to the low-*p* requests.

High-*p* request sequences can be used to increase a variety of behaviors, including academic, social, and self-care. This procedure can be implemented in three easy steps.

1. Create a pool of requests that generally result in compliance with at least 80% of opportunities. This pool is limited only by your imagination. Examples of potential high-*p* requests include the following:

   • High fives

- Brief preferred academic tasks (e.g., 1×1 digit problems, letter copying)
- Clapping
- Touching ears or nose

Initially the pool can be developed using caregiver input (e.g., asking, "What requests generally result in compliance?"). However, to be sure the requests result in compliance, intervenors should be sure to monitor compliance with these requests over the course of the intervention. In addition, the behaviors selected for the high-p should be very brief (i.e., less than 10 seconds in duration).

2. Deliver 3 to 4 high-p requests just prior to the low-p request.

3. Deliver verbal praise after compliance to both high-p and low-p requests.

With academic materials, high-p sequences can be implemented by designing them directly into academic materials. For example, a teacher may set up a worksheet with three preferred high-p math problems prior to each less preferred low-p problem:

$$
\begin{array}{cccc}
3 & 4 & 7 & 63 \\
+\,5 & +\,7 & +\,9 & +\,53 \\
\end{array}
$$

A teacher or parent similarly could use high-p sequences to facilitate transitions between academic tasks or medication taking.

1. High-p—"Give me five" ("Nice work!")
2. High-p—"Give me a hug" ("Great!")
3. High-p—"Touch your ear" ("Super!")
4. Low-p—"Take your medicine" ("Great work taking your medicine!")

Basic Principles Quiz 8

1. What is a contingency contract? What are some rules for a well-written contract?

_____

_____

_____

_____

_____

2. List four considerations that could help a new teacher or a parent more effectively deliver verbal praise.

_____

_____

_____

_____

_____

3. Mr. R's students seem to take forever to transition from snack time to science activities. Design a program using high-*p* sequences to facilitate the transition.

_____

_____

_____

_____

USING BEHAVIOR PRINCIPLES TO TEACH NEW BEHAVIORS

Basic behavior principles can be used to increase behaviors that are already in the learner's repertoire. Examples include increasing fluency of an academic task, the duration of conversations for an individual with a communication impairment, and the rate of appropriate positive self-statements. These same principles can be used to teach new behaviors. However, before these principles can be implemented as part of an instructional program, instructional control must be established.

Instructional Control

A necessary factor in teaching a skill is that the learner's behavior is under *instructional control*. This means that when the mentor gives an instruction, the learner follows the instruction. Think of how difficult it is to teach someone a behavior, such as how to use a new word processing program or a new digital camera, when the learner rejects the instructions of the mentor. People whose behavior is under instructional control have learned that if they follow written or verbal instructions (i.e., S^Ds), they are more likely to come in contact with reinforcement than they are if they disregard the instructions. To establish instructional control, mentors should reinforce instruction following behavior when it occurs. For example, suppose a child is running along the sides of a swimming pool and the father yells, "Jeannie, stop running." If the daughter stops running, the father should say, "Thank you for listening to me." The instructions of some people are followed, whereas those of others are usually ignored. The presence or absence of consequences causes the difference in the two outcomes. If a university has a deadline date for accepting applications for admission and enforces it, the school will have strong compliance with its policies. A teacher who gives homework assignments but does not grade the papers will likely find that few students do their homework. Some of the techniques presented earlier (e.g., verbal praise, contingency contracts, and high-p request sequences) can be used to increase instructional control.

> **KEY TERM:** *Instructional Control*
> Instructional control involves following directions in an instructional situation.

Opportunities To Respond and Three-Term Contingencies

People learn new behaviors by getting chances to respond and receiving feedback about whether their responses were appropriate. This unit of instruction is known as a *learning trial* or *three-term contingency.* The three-term contingency is essentially the ABCs of behavior already discussed (i.e., antecedents, behavior, and consequences). In a classroom this might consist of a teacher asking a question (first term), the students responding (second term), and the teacher giving the students feedback on their answers (third term). These units of instruction are important because they are related to academic success. Teachers who arrange more opportunities for students to complete three-term contingencies generally produce higher levels of student achievement. Unfortunately, too few teaching arrangements allow for the use of three-term contingencies. A visitor to a classroom might see one student reading aloud and the others staring into space or getting into trouble. A parent or supervisor might tell a child or employee how to perform a task but fail to provide the person with an opportunity to perform the behavior or give feedback as to how well the task was done.

If three-term contingencies are important in the learning process, how can they be provided? One way is through one-to-one tutoring programs, when one person who is competent at a skill teaches another person who has not yet mastered the skill. A second is through class-wide peer tutoring, in which all students take turns being tutor and learner. Another is through choral responding, in which a teacher asks a question, the group responds on a signal, and the teacher gives the students feedback on their answers. Preprinted response cards and whiteboards are also helpful. Teachers ask questions, the students write their answers on an erasable board, and the teacher provides feedback. Finally, computer-assisted instruction programs provide users with many opportunities to respond and offer immediate feedback on answers.

KEY TERM: *Three-Term Contingency*

A three-term contingency is composed of an antecedent, the behavior that follows, and the consequences that maintain the behavior. It is also called an instructional trial.

▶ **Assignment:** Devise a program by which one of the following individuals can use more three-term contingencies:

1. An employer teaching an employee accounting

2. A teacher instructing a student on social skills

3. A parent teaching a child to play soccer

The Role of Feedback and Reinforcement in Learning New Behaviors

When a reinforcer is delivered, two functions are served. The first and more obvious function is that the reinforcer motivates the person to continue performing the behavior. The second function is informing the person that he or she performed the behavior correctly. The latter function is *feedback* and refers to information on the quality or quantity of past performance. Evidence indicates that feedback alone can sometimes improve a person's behavior (Van Houten, 1980). For example, handing a student teacher a note indicating how many times she or he used praise for appropriate behavior can markedly improve the student teacher's rate of praise delivery. Also, a public graph of how many new calls a salesperson made or how many times a person engaged in aerobic exercise in a week can result in substantial improvement. The significant point here is that information alone is sometimes sufficient for change. Expensive and unwieldy reinforcers are not always necessary.

> **KEY TERM:** *Feedback*
> Feedback is information regarding the accuracy or quality of a behavior.

Shaping

It is easy to see how a reinforcement procedure can increase the occurrence of a behavior that already exists. If a secretary occasionally proofreads her work and her boss offers her a bonus for improved performance, she is likely to proofread at a higher rate. Using reinforcement to teach a new behavior is more complicated because one cannot reinforce a behavior that does not already exist. However, through a process known as *shaping*, reinforcement can be used to teach a new behavior.

Shaping takes advantage of the fact that almost any behavior occurs with variability, that is, it sometimes occurs one way, it next occurs in a slightly different way, and then it occurs in a third way. Shaping consists of reinforcing the existing behavior that comes closest to the desired (or *terminal*) behavior and then reinforcing closer and closer approximations to the terminal behavior. Once the terminal behavior is performed, it is reinforced until it occurs reliably. The behavior that is reinforced at the end is very different from the behavior that is reinforced at the beginning. This process is also known as *reinforcing successive approximations of the desired behavior.*

A mother who is trying to teach her young son to say "Mama" provides an example of how positive reinforcement can be used to shape behavior. In the beginning, any sound is reinforced. Later, a verbalization is reinforced only if it has the sound "m" in it. Next, "Ma" is reinforced, and still later it must be an intelligible "Mama." Sometimes shaping occurs naturally, such as learning to shift gears in a car with a standard transmission. A person's shifting behavior becomes more and more dexterous to avoid unpleasant sounds and a bucking sensation. This is an example of shaping using negative reinforcement.

Shaping can be achieved by following certain steps:

1. Define the terminal behavior.

2. Determine the initial behavior that the person can already perform (i.e., the closest approximation to the terminal behavior).

3. Break the target behavior into graduated steps, beginning with the behavior the person can already perform and ending with the terminal behavior.

4. Have the person perform each step toward the terminal behavior, reinforcing each one as it is achieved.

5. If a step is not performed, go back to an easier step until it is performed or further divide the existing steps into smaller steps.

6. Continue the procedure until the person is reliably performing the terminal behavior.

A person is likely to encounter two main difficulties in shaping a new behavior. One difficulty is caused by moving in steps that are too large. Therefore, the difference between one step in the shaping process and the next step should be small. The idea is to challenge someone but not to cause frustration. The second difficulty is not providing enough practice at a newly learned step before moving on to the next step. In teaching a new mathematical operation, for example, the teacher should provide a great deal of practice before moving to the next step.

KEY TERM: *Shaping*

Shaping involves systematically reinforcing successive approximations of a target behavior until the terminal behavior is reached.

▶ **Assignment:** Describe a shaping procedure for a behavior you wish to learn and implement the procedure. Report the results of your efforts.

_____

_____

_____

_____

_____

Basic Principles Quiz 9

1. Describe a shaping procedure for a student who can only sit still for 2 minutes in an hour. The desired terminal behavior is to sit still for 20 minutes.

    _____

    _____

    _____

    _____

    _____

2. Design a contingency contract to increase instructional control for a group of second-grade students.

    _____

    _____

    _____

3. Give three examples of three-term contingency instructional trials from a classroom.

	Antecedent	Behavior	Consequence
1.			
2.			
3.			

4. Name two functions of a reinforcer.

    _____

    _____

    _____

5. What is instructional control? How is it established?

_____

_____

_____

_____

_____

Modeling and Imitation

Commonly, people learn a new behavior or emit an existing one more frequently by imitating the behavior of someone else. *Imitation* is the process by which people learn a behavior by observing another person perform the behavior. The person originally performing the behavior is known as the *model*. During the observation period, the learner neither performs the behavior nor receives a reinforcer. He simply learns through the process of observing. Later, when he exhibits the behavior, his behavior may be reinforced.

Clearly, imitation is a common and powerful means of acquiring new behaviors. Children rapidly learn speech by imitating the language patterns of their parents. In so doing, they often use expressions and speak with inflections similar to those of their parents. When children become adolescents, their hair and clothing styles closely resemble those of other teenagers. Sometimes children imitate undesirable behaviors of their friends and become consumers of cigarettes and alcohol at a young age. Indeed, many parents complain that their children imitate inappropriate behavior more readily than appropriate behavior. When a supervisor or parent says, "Watch how I do this," she is teaching a behavior through modeling. Teachers frequently perform a complex operation, such as balancing a chemical equation, in full view of students, so that students will more readily imitate the process. Often, teachers encourage children to look at a written model of a mathematical operation so that they will use similar steps to solve a comparable problem.

A number of factors increase the likelihood of behavior imitation. If the model's behavior is frequently reinforced, especially with large amounts of reinforcement, imitation is likely to occur. Also, simple behaviors are more likely than complex behaviors to be imitated. Certain characteristics of the model influence the probability of imitation occurring. Thus, prestigious models and models of the same gender, race, and age are likely to be imitated, a fact well known to advertisers.

KEY TERM: *Modeling*

Modeling involves demonstrating a behavior.

KEY TERM: *Imitation*

Imitation involves performing a behavior that is modeled.

▶ **Assignment:** Describe three beneficial and three detrimental instances of imitation common in your environment.

_____

_____

_____

_____

_____

_____

Prompting and Fading

A means of accelerating the learning process is to use prompts. A prompt is an S^D and can take the form of a hint, a modeled behavior, underlined words, verbal emphasis, physical assistance, and so on. It is important to use the appropriate type of prompt. When a teacher asks, "Who was the president during the American Civil War?" and is pointing to a picture of Abraham Lincoln, he or she is giving a prompt that makes it more likely the students will get the answer to the question correct. These correct answers, even with prompts, are reinforced, making the correct answer more likely to occur in the future. There are two broad categories of prompts: stimulus and response.

Stimulus Prompts

For *stimulus prompts* the instructor changes the antecedent in the three-term contingency to make a response more likely to occur. Some common examples of stimulus prompts include the following:

- Using a highlighter to make the operation sign (e.g., plus sign) more salient in a math problem
- Pairing a picture with a common word (e.g., pairing a picture of a milk carton with the word *milk*)
- Using a list to guide responses (e.g., a note for the store)
- Underlining key sentences in a textbook
- Using a jig or template when completing an assembly task

The key to an effective stimulus prompt is to select a prompt that requires the person to attend to the S^D. In the example in the previous section, the teacher asked the question and pointed to the picture of Abraham Lincoln. In this case the student had to attend to the question (S^D) in order to give a correct answer. Sometimes teachers give prompts that do not require students to attend to the S^D. For example, if the teacher in the example asked, "Was Abraham Lincoln the president during the American Civil War?" and nodded, the students would probably get the answer correct. However, the prompt did not require the students to know anything about the question. As a result, the students are less likely to pair the question ("Was Abraham Lincoln president during the American Civil War?") with the correct answer (Abraham Lincoln).

Response Prompts

For *response prompts* the antecedent remains the same. However, the instructor provides assistance to the behavior part of the three-term contingency. There are several common types of response prompts.

Verbal Prompts. *Verbal prompts* in the form of spoken instructions sometimes are used when a new behavior is being established. If the behavior is properly reinforced, the verbal instructions can often be discontinued gradually and the behavior will continue. This is what happens when a teacher establishes routines in the classroom or when an office manager introduces a new clerk to office procedures. The first day, someone gives instructions, and the person receiving instructions emits the behavior that is reinforced. The next day, in the same situation, the instructions are repeated, the behavior occurs, and then it is reinforced. The following day someone gives abbreviated instructions, the behavior occurs, and then it is reinforced. Soon it is no longer necessary for the teacher or office manager to issue instructions because the S^{D}s provided by the situation are sufficient to prompt the behavior. As long as enough reinforcement is provided, the behavior will be maintained.

Gestural Prompts. *Gestures*, expressive movements of the body or limbs to convey an idea, are frequently used to prompt behaviors. Sometimes, gestures are used as prompts to occasion behavior after verbal prompts have been faded. Gestures such as a nod or a motion to go away or come forward also may be faded once the behavior is well established.

Physical Prompts. Sometimes shaping, modeling, and using verbal or visual prompts are ineffective in helping to initiate a new behavior. In such situations it may be necessary to physically prompt the desired behavior. That is, initially it may be necessary for the instructor to actually place his or her hands on the learner and guide the behavior. We usually help initiate behavior by using physical prompts when we are teaching a person to ride a bicycle, golf, or tie shoes.

Fading

Once a behavior has been learned, it is desirable to gradually remove the prompts, which is a process known as *fading*. The purpose of fading is to get a behavior to occur under normal environmental conditions rather than having a person depend on prompts provided by other people. For example, we want a child to put on a coat because it is cold outside, not because her mother told her to do so. Thus, fading produces independent responding.

Note two key points about fading prompts. First, try starting an instructional program with the weakest prompt possible and move to stronger prompts as needed. It is often easier to fade weak (e.g., verbal) prompts than strong (e.g., physical) prompts. Second, some individuals with more significant disabilities may always require some level of prompting to complete a task. For example, Michael may always require a diagram of table settings to help him set the table.

KEY TERM: *Prompt*

A prompt involves assistance that makes it more likely that a behavior will be performed correctly.

> **KEY TERM:** *Fading*
> Fading is the gradual and systematic removal of a prompt that results in more independent responding.

▶ **Assignment:** Suggest a fading procedure that will get a child who sleeps only with a light on to sleep in darkness.

_____

_____

_____

_____

Name two other prompts you once attended to but which are no longer needed to help you make correct responses.

_____

_____

_____

_____

People often confuse shaping and fading. In the case of shaping, a person is trying to teach an entirely new behavior. In the case of fading, the desired behavior already exists. In fading, the task of the instructor, therefore, is to get the same behavior to occur under new conditions (e.g., without instructions or hints). In the shaping process, what the learner does changes (e.g., drawing a circle differently). In fading, what the teacher does changes (e.g., gives fewer or different types of prompts).

Finally, in shaping, the teacher manipulates consequences; in fading she or he manipulates antecedents.

Behavior Chains

Most human responses are not solitary acts. Rather, they are complex behaviors consisting of numerous, simpler behaviors. Behaviors such as getting ready for work, going shopping, or reading a book can be broken into many smaller behaviors. A *behavior chain* is the sequence of behaviors that make up a more complex behavior. The reinforcer that follows the final behavior maintains the succession of behaviors. Discriminative stimuli also play an important role in behavior chains because they signal the next behavior in the response chain.

Consider making a peanut butter and jelly sandwich, for example. This task can be broken into six basic steps:

1. Get out two slices of bread.
2. Get out the peanut butter and jelly.
3. Get out a knife.
4. Spread the peanut butter and jelly onto the bread.
5. Put the slices of bread together.
6. Eat the sandwich.

For this chain of behaviors, each response serves as an S^D for subsequent steps and as a conditioned reinforcer for previous steps. Getting out the knife serves as an S^D for spreading the peanut butter and jelly onto the bread, and spreading the peanut butter and jelly onto the bread serves as a conditioned reinforcer for getting out the knife. Each step in the sequence serves as a conditioned reinforcer because it is connected to the final step (eating the sandwich) through pairing. In this way, long and complex response chains are maintained.

Consider a more complex example. A person who wishes to go from his office to his home emits many behaviors. In the process of leaving his office, each step he makes brings him closer to his car in the parking lot. These steps reinforce the previous steps and are S^Ds for the next step. He emits more behaviors as he gets into his car, starts the engine, and drives toward home. As long as he makes the correct turns, his behavior is reinforced. In this way, he finally arrives home, a behavior that is reinforced by watching the evening news, eating dinner, and any other reinforcers available in the home.

Chains depend on the fact that S^Ds become conditioned reinforcers for the responses that precede them. A simple example of this can be seen in a teenager sitting in the living room. She suddenly feels a hunger pang. The hunger pang serves as an S^D for her to get up and walk into the kitchen. When she gets to the kitchen, she sees the refrigerator door. This new S^D reinforces the response of walking to the kitchen and acts as a cue to open the door. Opening the door is reinforced by the presence of a big, juicy apple. The process continues as shown in Table 2.

Often new behaviors can be taught by chaining a series of existing behaviors into novel sequences. Thus, a child might know every word in a poem but must learn to recite the words in the correct order. A person might have the subskills to perform an operation on the computer but must put them together in the correct order to perform the operation correctly.

One issue in teaching a behavior through chaining is the order in which one teaches the subskills. The most obvious means is to teach the initial subskill, then the second, and so on. This process, called *forward chaining*, is typically followed when a mother teaches her child the alphabet. First she teaches the letter *A*. After the letter *A* is mastered, she moves on to the letter *B* and so forth. An alternative to this process is to use *backward chaining*, in which the last link is taught first, followed by the next-to-last link, and so forth. This method probably seems like a strange way to teach, but it is the preferred manner

TABLE 2
Behavior Chain for Eating an Apple

S^D	R (Response)	S^D and Reinforcer
Hunger pangs in stomach	Walks to kitchen	Sees refrigerator
Walks over and opens door	Sees apple	Picks up apple and raises it to mouth
Feels apple on teeth	Bites and chews apple	Tastes and feels good

in some cases. For example, in teaching a young child to tie his or her shoe, a parent may complete all the steps and ask the child to "pull the bunny ears tight" to complete last step. Once the child is proficient in the last step, the parent asks the child to perform the last two steps of shoe tying: "pull the loop through the hole and pull the bunny ears tight." This process continues until the child independently ties his or her shoes. The advantage in backward chaining is that people have many S^Ds for the next response in the chain and have the reinforcer of a completed task in front of them for each successful effort. Another way to teach a behavior chain is *total task presentation.* Unlike forward and backward chaining, where only one step is presented at a time, in total task presentation each step of the task is taught during a given instructional session. Total task presentation often results in instructional sessions that last longer than other methods, but it requires fewer overall sessions to learn a chain of behaviors. However, error rates can be high because each step is presented every day. Forward or backward chaining can be used to limit the number of errors. In choosing forward or backward chaining, a teacher should determine where the easier links of behavior appear and then teach those links first.

People are so dependent on some chains of behavior that if the chain is disrupted, they become thoroughly disoriented. Try singing a song starting with the second verse or reciting a poem starting in the middle. Similarly, when a person faces a short detour on the way home from work, he or she might have difficulty finding the way home.

KEY TERM: *Behavior Chain*

A behavior chain is a series of discrete behaviors that forms a complex skill. Each link in the chain becomes an S^D for the subsequent step and acts as a conditioned reinforcer for the previous step.

Generalization and Discrimination

Generalization refers to the degree to which a behavior that has been reinforced in one situation will occur in other situations. For example, a person might learn to use a word processor on one type of computer at work and then competently exhibit the same skill on another computer at home. A child might learn that a rose and a tulip are flowers and then identify a violet as a flower. Without generalization, people would have to learn each new task from scratch. Fortunately, people can apply what they have learned in the past to new situations. People learn which behavior is appropriate and likely to be reinforced in one situation. People also learn that the same behavior is likely to be appropriate and reinforced in situations that are similar, though not identical. Thus, people are not faced with the task of learning exactly what to do every time they encounter situations that differ in minor details. The practice of schooling children makes the assumption that generalization will occur. For example, it is assumed that if a child learns to read in school, the child will also read in other settings. If this were not the case, the usefulness of schools would be doubtful.

Discrimination, the opposite of generalization, refers to the fact that certain behaviors reliably occur in some situations but not in others. A student who behaves appropriately in the presence of her teacher but inappropriately for a substitute teacher has made a discrimination. The same is true for a person who is punctual when the boss is in but tardy when the boss is on vacation. It is common to see children behave one way in the presence of their father and another in their mother's presence. Were it not for discrimination, human lives would be chaotic. Because most people learn to discriminate, they typically do not emit behaviors in situations in which those behaviors are inappropriate.

Sometimes the occurrence of generalization is desirable, and sometimes it is not. A desirable case of generalization occurs when a person learns to serve a tennis ball on one court and then exhibits the same skill on other courts. An undesirable case of generalization occurs when a child runs freely in the schoolyard, is reinforced for that behavior, and then also runs around the classroom. The same is true for discrimination. A desirable case of discrimination involves dressing professionally for work but dressing casually at home. An undesirable case of discrimination occurs when a child exhibits fluent speech for a therapist who reinforces such behavior but is not fluent in any other environments.

Specific operations can bring about generalization and discrimination (Stokes & Baer, 1977). Strategies for achieving generalization include teaching behaviors that are useful in many situations, teaching the behavior in several environments, teaching the behavior to a fluent level, varying instructions and reinforcers, and using social reinforcers. Discrimination can be achieved best by reinforcing a behavior in the desired environment and not reinforcing that same behavior in undesirable situations.

KEY TERM: *Generalization*

Generalization involves performing a behavior in environments that differ from the teaching environment.

> **KEY TERM:** *Discrimination*
> Discrimination involves performing a behavior only in specific situations.

Basic Principles Quiz 10

1. Describe three factors that increase the probability that a modeled behavior will be imitated.

   _____

   _____

   _____

   _____

   _____

2. Distinguish among forward chaining, backward chaining, and total task presentation.

   _____

   _____

   _____

   _____

   _____

3. Distinguish between shaping and fading.

   _____

   _____

   _____

_____

_____

_____

Barb was learning to fly a plane but was having difficulty handling the throttle. When her instructor said, "Ease back on the throttle," Barb looked bewildered and tense and pulled back on the control column. Her instructor then repeated his instructions and demonstrated pulling back on the throttle. When Barb tried it the next time, she pulled the throttle back so rapidly that the engine died. After restarting the engine, the instructor repeated his instruction and guided Barb's hand in easing back on the throttle, praising her by saying, "That's good." Gradually, he ceased guiding Barb's hand as he gave instructions and praise. By the end of the lesson, when the instructor said "Ease back on the throttle," Barb was doing so promptly and smoothly. The engine noises decreased to a steady purr, and the instructor said, "Great!"

4. Initially, Barb's responses were not under

_____.

5. How did generalization cause her problems?

_____

_____

_____

_____

6. The instructor's directions, therefore, were not an _____ for easing back on the throttle.

7. Was modeling alone effective in this case? _____

8. What procedures were finally necessary to teach the correct response to Barb?

    _____

9. By the end of the lesson, what two discriminations had Barb learned as far as airplane controls are concerned?

    a. _____

    b. _____

10. Diagram at least six parts of the chain of responses and S^Ds involved when Barb eased back on the throttle upon instruction.

S^D	R (Response)	S^D (Reinforcer)	R (Response)	Reinforcer or S^D (Reinforcer)

PROCEDURES FOR DECREASING BEHAVIOR

Until now, we have discussed procedures to get existing behaviors to occur more frequently or to create new behaviors where a need exists. Sometimes, however, people are faced with unacceptable behaviors and need to find procedures that will decrease occurrence of those behaviors. Examples include a boy who frequently hits his sister, a student who teases a classmate, and an employer who publicly ridicules her workers. This section discusses procedures that can be used to decrease or eliminate unacceptable behavior.

A Hierarchy of Behavior Reduction Techniques

There are two general categories of behavior reduction techniques. The first category consists of nonpunishment procedures, whereas the second category consists of punishment procedures. These behavior reduction techniques are further arranged into a hierarchy (Alberto & Troutman, 2003; see Table 3). Use of this hierarchy ensures that behavior change agents will start with less intrusive approaches before moving to more intrusive approaches.

Behavior reduction procedures should be used only after more positive interventions have been exhausted. The hierarchy shown in Table 3 should be used as a guideline. Obviously, common sense should prevail in situations that warrant behavior reduction programs. Here are several other questions that should be considered before using a behavior reduction procedure:

1. Is the behavior change important for the student (i.e., not just convenient for others)?

TABLE 3
Hierarchy of Behavior Reduction Techniques

Level	Definition	Examples
1	Use of reinforcement to decrease inappropriate behaviors by reinforcing more appropriate behaviors	DRL DRO DRI DRA
2	Techniques based on withholding reinforcers for a previously reinforced behavior	Extinction
3	Techniques that remove desirable stimuli to reduce behavior	Response cost Time out
4	Interventions that use aversive stimuli to reduce behavior	A stern verbal reprimand Cleaning a desk after writing on it with a marker

DRL = differential reinforcement of low rate of response; DRO = differential reinforcement of other behavior; DRI = differential reinforcement of incompatible behavior; DRA = differential reinforcement of alternative behavior.

2. Have you reviewed the regulations of your organization regarding behavior reduction techniques?

3. Are you trying to replace the inappropriate behavior with a functional alternative?

4. Is a medical problem causing the inappropriate behavior (e.g., ear infection)?

Decreasing Behavior Through Reinforcement

Because reinforcement was previously described as a means to increase behavior, it might seem surprising that it is also a means of decreasing behavior. Yet, there are some ways in which reinforcement can be used in this manner. One procedure, known as *differential reinforcement of low rate of response* (DRL), provides reinforcers to an individual or a group when the target behavior occurs below a specified level. For example, a father might allow his daughter to stay up an extra 15 minutes if she leaves fewer than four items of clothing on the floor on a given day. A teacher might inform her students that they can watch a favorite DVD if they perform fewer than 20 out-of-seat behaviors in a morning. As the behavior improves, the criterion can be gradually reduced to 18, 15, 12, and so forth until a set goal is reached.

> **KEY TERM:** *Differential Reinforcement of Low Rate of Response (DRL)*
> DRL involves systematically reinforcing lower and lower rates of a target behavior in an effort to decrease, but not eliminate, that behavior.

A second means of decreasing behavior through reinforcement is to use *differential reinforcement of other behavior* (DRO). With this procedure, a reinforcer is delivered if a specified behavior does not occur for a stated period of time. Suppose a child frequently sucks her thumb. On a DRO 10 schedule, she would receive a reinforcer if she refrained from sucking her thumb for 10 minutes. After the delivery of a reinforcer, a new 10-minute cycle would then begin. If she sucked her thumb before 10 minutes passed, the timer would be reset and a new 10-minute cycle would begin. The program can be faded by slowly and systematically increasing the requirements for a reinforcer. For example, after the child has consistently refrained from thumb sucking for 10 minutes, the DRO schedule could be increased to 12 minutes, 14 minutes, and so on.

KEY TERM: *Differential Reinforcement of Other Behavior (DRO)*
DRO involves delivering a reinforcer when a person refrains from engaging in a behavior for a set period of time in an effort to eliminate that behavior.

A third way of reducing behavior through reinforcement is by *differential reinforcement of incompatible behavior* (DRI). If an employee is often late, for example, he can be praised or receive a complimentary note when he is punctual (i.e., tardiness and punctuality are incompatible). In a classroom, the best way to reinforce incompatible behavior is to keep students engaged academically. When students are fully occupied by responding correctly to academic tasks, they cannot misbehave.

KEY TERM: *Differential Reinforcement of Incompatible Behavior (DRI)*
The DRI procedure involves reinforcing responses that are incompatible with the target behavior in an effort to eliminate the target behavior.

Another way to decrease problem behavior is to teach a new behavior to replace the maladaptive response. In *differential reinforcement of alternative behavior* (DRA), a behavior that serves the same purpose as the maladaptive response is taught and reinforced. As a result of this procedure, the individual typically begins to engage in the appropriate behavior more and more often. The new appropriate behavior replaces the problem behavior. For example, a student may have a tantrum to get attention from his teacher. The teacher could teach and reinforce the behavior of hand raising to get attention instead. If the teacher only attends to the new behavior, the student will begin to raise his hand more often and have tantrums less often. One key to using DRA is to be sure to reinforce a behavior that is more efficient and accesses reinforcers more quickly than the inappropriate behavior.

KEY TERM: *Differential Reinforcement of Alternative Behavior (DRA)*
DRA involves teaching and reinforcing an appropriate behavior that can be used in place of the targeted inappropriate behavior.

▶ **Assignment:** Identify an inappropriate behavior exhibited by an employee, domestic partner, or child and use one of the reinforcement procedures described in this section to reduce it.

_____

_____

_____

Decreasing Behavior Through Extinction

Sometimes an inappropriate behavior has been frequently reinforced in the past. For example, a mother may have reinforced her son's whining by giving the child what he wanted, or a teacher may have reinforced a student's profanity by showing anger. In such cases, a person can cease reinforcing the behavior and may find that the behavior occurs less frequently. People will stop working if they are not paid and will stop supporting a sports team that seldom wins. Often the process consists of planned ignoring of inappropriate behavior.

> **KEY TERM:** *Extinction*
> Extinction involves withholding a reinforcer to eliminate a behavior.

People trying to eliminate a behavior using an extinction procedure should go through the following steps:

1. Define the target behavior.

2. Collect baseline, or preintervention, data to see how often behavior occurs.

3. Observe the consequences of the behavior to determine what might be reinforcing the behavior.

4. Arrange for the removal of the reinforcing consequences (e.g., remove attention by ignoring the behavior).

5. Continue to record the occurrence of the behavior to see if it decreases to low rates.

6. If behavior does not decrease, be sure that you (a) located the reinforcer that is maintaining the behavior and (b) eliminated all sources of the reinforcement for the targeted behavior.

These steps notwithstanding, extinction is not always easy to achieve. The process can be slow, but the speed can be increased when extinction is used in conjunction with a procedure that reinforces desirable behavior, such as DRA. That is, if a parent is no longer attending to a child's whining, she can reinforce requests made in a pleasant manner. A teacher who is no longer showing that he is upset by a student's profanity can praise the youngster for speaking properly.

In addition to being a slow process, extinction can involve a number of other problems. First, most people find it difficult not to react to inappropriate behavior. In addition, even if one person stops reacting to a problem, it is possible that other people will continue to attend to the behavior. Also, a behavior undergoing extinction may occur more frequently before it decreases in rate. This process is known as *extinction burst* and may prove intolerable to some people who, consequently, will ultimately give in and reinforce the behavior. In addition, behaviors that have decreased in rate tend to suddenly recur. This recurrence of the behavior is called *spontaneous recovery* and it might prove troublesome for people who are no longer prepared for it. Another problem is that the person whose behavior is being ignored might respond with aggression, crying, or frustration. Finally, some behaviors, such as self-injury or property destruction, are too dangerous or expensive to ignore.

Because of the extinction curve (an increase and then a sharp decrease in the behavior), it is important for persons using this procedure to record data on the behavior. Parents who see the behavior change as predicted are much more likely to carry through with the procedure than they would if they were left to their own devices. This is especially true if their son or daughter is very skilled at getting attention by crying, screaming, kicking, coughing, and so forth, with increasing intensity because of a history of having had the target behavior reinforced by the well-meaning but distraught parents.

In spite of these problems, the process has some benefits and can be used under carefully controlled conditions. For example, extinction could be used with a child who cries for attention every night when put to bed. This application involves few dangers, and it usually works after a few nights. The process also has the advantage of not programming any unpleasant consequences that occur with punishment procedures.

Resistance to extinction is an outcome that can be measured by the number of behaviors a person performs after reinforcement is terminated. The rate at which extinction occurs depends on the kind of reinforcement schedule used. Behaviors on an intermittent schedule of reinforcement show more resistance to extinction (i.e., will extinguish more slowly) than behaviors on a continuous reinforcement schedule do. Vending and slot machines provide an excellent example of how people respond on various schedules of reinforcement. A vending machine generally distributes reinforcers on a continuous schedule. A person attempting to buy a drink will make very few attempts before he or she figures out that the vending machine is broken and consequently stops putting money into the machine. However, a slot machine delivers reinforcers on an intermittent schedule. It would take much longer for a person to learn that a slot machine is malfunctioning. As a result of this intermittent schedule of reinforcement, a person will persist much longer in placing money into a broken slot machine than a broken vending machine. Also, variable schedules of reinforcement produce more resistance to extinction than fixed schedules do because of the unpredictability of reinforcement on variable schedules. Therefore, an abandoned extinction procedure can make a behavior more resistant to intervention. Starting and then discontinuing an extinction intervention sets up an intermittent reinforcement schedule for the inappropriate behavior. The continual pattern of withholding and then reinforcing, which occurs when you start and stop the procedure, may make the inappropriate behavior more difficult to change. The bottom line is that parents and teachers should be sure that they can control all sources of reinforcement for the behavior and can ride out extinction bursts and spontaneous recovery before beginning the procedure. If you anticipate needing to start and stop the extinction intervention, you may want to select another technique. Figure 8 shows a hypothetical extinction curve for a boy who engaged in frequent tantrums until his parents began to systematically ignore his tantrums.

> ▶ **Assignment:** Each time Marsha cries after being put to bed, her parents come to her room, comfort her, and get her a drink of water. Tony's parents, on the other hand, often go to him

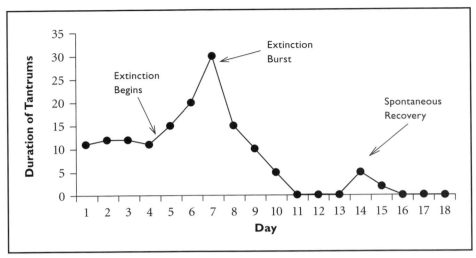

Figure 8. Example of an extinction curve.

when he cries, but sometimes they let him cry a long time before they respond to him. On some nights they let him "cry it out" without ever going to him. One night, both sets of parents decide that they will henceforth let the children cry until they fall asleep. Other things being equal, which child will become a good sleeper first? Why?

_____

_____

_____

Decreasing Behavior Through Punishment

Unfortunately, ignoring inappropriate behavior and reinforcing appropriate behavior do not always produce the desired reduction in unacceptable behavior. An effective but controversial means of reducing behavior is to use punishment. A *punisher* is any consequence of behavior that reduces the future rate of that behavior (Alberto & Troutman, 2003; Azrin & Holz, 1966). Suppose a student taunts another child. If the teacher requires the student to sit in a corner of the room for 5 minutes each time the behavior occurs and the rate of occurrence of the inappropriate behavior decreases, punishment has occurred. If the rate stays the same or increases, punishment has not occurred.

Punishment is not the same as negative reinforcement. In the case of negative reinforcement, a person responds at a high rate to avoid or escape an unpleasant event. With punishment, a person responds less frequently to avoid the unpleasant event. Negative reinforcement produces an increase in behavior. Punishment produces a decrease in behavior.

Research has revealed that several factors influence the use of punishment procedures (Azrin & Holz, 1966). First, the more intense the punisher is, the more effective the punishment is. Also, it is better to use an intense punisher at the start and gradually reduce its intensity than to proceed in the opposite manner, which unfortunately is the common tendency. Also, if people can avoid punishment through apologies, lies, or "one more chance," the punishment procedure will be ineffective. The most important thing to do is to combine reinforcement of appropriate behavior with punishment for inappropriate behavior. If a person is reprimanded for absenteeism, he should be complimented for coming to work. If a child is required to go to sleep early for breaking her younger brother's toys, she should receive a reinforcer when she treats his toys properly. The reinforcement component teaches the correct behavior and results in a quicker and greater reduction in the undesirable behavior. It also allows you to use a less intense punisher and still be effective.

One of the major concerns about punishment techniques is that they can result in undesirable side effects. Indeed, research has found this to be true sometimes (Newsom, Favell, & Rincover, 1983). Undesirable side effects can involve aggression toward the person administering punishment or toward others in the environment (i.e., scapegoating). A person receiving punishment might cry, scream, pout, or try to avoid the person or environment where punishment occurs (e.g., by "skipping"). Such occurrences are relatively rare and can be averted by combining positive reinforcement for appropriate behavior with punishment for inappropriate behavior.

As indicated earlier, the use of punishment techniques has been widely criticized. Some in the field claim that only positive techniques should be used in behavior change. One issue, however, is that the natural environment automatically punishes some behaviors. This type of punishment occurs when we walk into walls or spill boiling water on our hands. Still, the question remains whether teachers, employers, and parents should program punishment. Probably, this is sometimes necessary. Indeed, people who claim that others should not use punishment procedures engage in fierce attacks on those who do. The best way to proceed is to use frequent positive reinforcement but also to occasionally use properly applied punishment as a last resort. The next sections discuss three punishment techniques that can be helpful and humanely employed.

KEY TERM: *Punishment*

Punishment is the process by which the consequences of a behavior reduce the probability that a given behavior will occur in the future.

Reprimands

A common and acceptable form of punishment is the *reprimand*, which is any expression of disapproval and can consist of verbal disapproval, a pointed finger, or a critical facial expression (Van Houten & Doleys, 1983). Examples of reprimands include a father telling his son, "Don't talk to your sister that way"; a teacher telling a class to "Keep quiet"; or an employer admonishing an employee to stop coming to work late. Verbal reprimands should be delivered right after a behavior occurs; should be delivered privately, whenever possible; and should be brief. Verbal reprimands should specify the undesirable behavior and should not demean the recipient's character. Thus, it is more humane to say, "What you just did was inconsiderate," than, "You are inconsiderate." In other words, focus more on the behavior and not so much on the person. Reprimands for inappropriate behavior should be combined with praise for appropriate behavior.

KEY TERM: *Reprimand*

A reprimand is a verbal or gestural expression of disapproval.

Response Cost

Response cost involves removing certain amounts of a person's or group's reinforcers following an unacceptable behavior. Reinforcers that can be removed include tokens, free time, money, points, and so forth. Response cost is often carried out in conjunction with a token reinforcement program. In one form of response cost, people are given free reinforcers and can lose them contingent on each undesirable behavior. In a second form of response cost, people can earn reinforcers for correct behavior and lose reinforcers for incorrect behavior. The popular television quiz show *Jeopardy* is an example of the second type of response-cost procedure. Contestants earn money for answering questions correctly and lose money when they give incorrect answers.

There are numerous examples of response cost in our environment. When the government fines its citizens for a traffic violation, it is using a response-cost procedure. The same is true for a cellular telephone company that charges extra for calls that exceed a customer's allotted minutes. Parents can also use response cost. A child can be offered 10 extra minutes of staying-up time each night. Each time the child teases his sister, however, he loses 2 minutes of the extra time. If he has no extra minutes left, the child can be required to go to sleep 2 minutes earlier than usual for each additional misbehavior.

Teachers can also make use of response-cost procedures. One of the most powerful procedures we have encountered is the use of response cost with an entire group of students. For example, a teacher offers her students 12 extra minutes of free time. She writes the number of minutes on the chalkboard in this form:

Minutes of Free Time

12 11 10 9 8 7 6 5 4 3 2 1 0

Each time a student breaks a specified rule (e.g., leaving seat without permission), the entire group loses 1 minute of free time. Thus, if three rules are broken, the teacher would mark off 3 minutes on the board:

Minutes of Free Time

~~12~~ ~~11~~ ~~10~~ 9 8 7 6 5 4 3 2 1 0

When the time is over, the group gets the amount of free time that remains. In this case, three rules were broken and, thus, 9 minutes of free time remain.

Response cost can also be used to improve an academic skill. Students, for example, can earn a point for each problem done correctly and lose a point for each error. The points left over can be used to purchase back-up reinforcers. A college professor once devised a means for preventing some students from dominating classroom discussions. Each student started the day with three markers and was required to remove a marker for each question the student asked. When he or she used up the three markers, that student's contributions to the class were over.

The advantages of response-cost procedures are that they are easy to apply, often produce immediate and major decreases in inappropriate behavior, and produce long-lasting effects. The disadvantages of response cost are that sometimes people become upset when they lose a reinforcer, that people "give up" when all their reinforcers are gone, and that too much attention is given to inappropriate behavior. To combat the last problem, people using response cost should be sure to reinforce appropriate behavior when it occurs.

KEY TERM: *Response Cost*

Response cost is a procedure whereby reinforcers are removed in an effort to decrease a target behavior.

Time Out

Time out from positive reinforcement, or *time out* as it more commonly called, is a popular punishment technique with both parents and teachers. It is also one of the most misused behavior change techniques. When applied correctly, time out can be an effective way to decrease problem behavior. However, when applied incorrectly, use of time out may actually act to reinforce the very behavior we wish to eliminate. The procedure involves having a person experience a less reinforcing environment for a period of time following an inappropriate behavior. According to this broad definition, the existing environment can be made less reinforcing by, for example, asking a student to turn off her MP3 player for 10 minutes or removing a person from the present environment and placing him in a less appealing one, such as the back of the room.

We see examples of time out across many environments. In athletics, for example, coaches take players out of a game for several minutes for poor play. In ice hockey, players are required to sit in the penalty box for a period of time for breaking a rule. In home situations, a parent may require a child to sit in a chair for a few minutes following an unacceptable behavior. A student who throws food or pushes schoolmates in the cafeteria might be required to spend the rest of the lunch period sitting alone.

Schools have sometimes made formal use of time-out procedures. In one arrangement, known as *contingent observation,* a student must sit in a corner of the classroom for a period of time but can observe and participate in classroom assignments. Contingent observation is advantageous in that the student does not miss valuable instruction time but is momentarily ineligible for reinforcers. In another arrangement, *exclusion time out,* the student faces the corner of the room for a specified period of time but cannot participate in any classroom activities.

Three matters concerning time out merit attention. First, time out is effective only to the extent that the normal (i.e., time-in) environment is more reinforcing than the time-out environment. Thus, teachers must attempt to make their class the most reinforcing event in the student's day. Students who are removed from boring, poorly managed classrooms for misbehaving quickly learn that their inappropriate behavior can be used to escape such environments through negative reinforcement. Similarly, parents should not be surprised if sending a child to his or her room is an ineffective procedure if the child's room contains diversions such as a CD player, a television, and a telephone. (Prohibiting the use of these devices during time out might be helpful.)

A second issue is that the purpose of time out is to punish inappropriate behavior. It is not a time to counsel or console a person. The purpose of a time-out procedure is to deprive a person of her usual reinforcers, not to provide new ones.

Finally, in a third time-out arrangement, *seclusion time out,* the student is placed in a separate room in the school. Many people see seclusion time out as an extreme procedure. Therefore, it should not be used until reasonable alternatives have been ruled out, unless school district policies are carefully followed and all relevant parties agree to the necessity and nature of the time-out procedure. This discussion should include parents, the teacher, and the school's principal.

KEY TERM: *Time Out*

Time out involves removing the individual from a reinforcing environment in an effort to decrease a target behavior.

Basic Principles Quiz 11

1. Give one example of each level of the hierarchy of behavior reduction strategies.

   _____

   _____

   _____

   _____

   _____

2. Mark is a child who constantly irritates his mother until she gets angry with him. Mom suspects that the attention she gives to Mark is reinforcing the behavior. She therefore tries to extinguish the behavior by ignoring Mark's irritating comments. What are three things that Mark's mother should expect to happen?

   _____

   _____

   _____

   _____

   _____

3. What is resistance to extinction? Which schedule of reinforcement should produce the greatest resistance to extinction?

_____

_____

_____

_____

_____

4. What is a DRL schedule of reinforcement? Describe how you would use DRL to reduce out-of-seat behaviors in a classroom.

_____

_____

_____

_____

_____

5. Define *extinction* and *punishment*. How are extinction and punishment alike? How are they different?

_____

_____

_____

_____

_____

6. How are negative reinforcement and punishment different? Give an example of each procedure.

_____

_____

_____

_____

_____

7. Describe three factors that would make a punishment procedure more effective.

_____

_____

_____

_____

_____

8. When punishing an inappropriate behavior, why is it also important to reinforce an appropriate behavior? Describe a program that does this.

_____

_____

_____

_____

_____

9. Describe the conditions under which you would use a punishment procedure.

_____

_____

_____

_____

_____

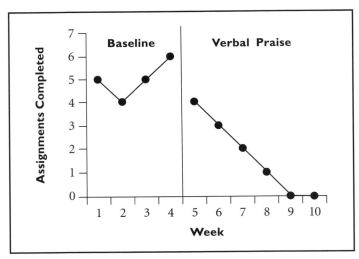

Figure 9. Assignment completion for Mitch.

10. Mrs. E gives Mitch verbal praise every time he completes his homework assignment. Is verbal praise a reinforcer or a punisher based on the data shown in Figure 9? Justify your answer.

_____

_____

_____

_____

_____

_____

_____

MOVING BEYOND BASIC PRINCIPLES

Application of Strategies

To this point we have discussed some basic principles of behavior. These principles are important because they provide the foundation for behavior change programs. Knowing how to increase known behaviors, teach new behaviors, and decrease inappropriate behaviors are important first steps in developing behavior change programs. In this section, we present steps to help you design and implement behavior change strategies.

Steps of Behavior Change

Axelrod (2003) presented a series of steps that practitioners should follow in developing a behavior change program. When combined with the basic principles of behavior, these steps provide a more systematic way to change behavior.

Step 1: Identify the Behavior Targeted for Intervention

The first step in developing a behavior change program is to identify the behavior targeted for intervention. This step is sometimes completed too quickly, often with a "knee-jerk" response. As practitioners and parents, we typically identify those behaviors that annoy us most as the behaviors that should be changed. For example, a child may continually ask, "Why?" in response to parental requests, or a student may talk with her neighbor during math class. However, we need to go beyond our list of pet peeves and ask what is best for the individual. Asking "why" questions may help that child learn more about the world. Although it may be annoying for an adult to answer question after question, the child may ultimately benefit from the answers. Similarly, the student who talks to a neighbor during math may be seeking additional information about a difficult math concept. Reducing this behavior may close one important avenue of student learning. Decreasing behaviors in both of these instances may suit the needs of the parent or teacher, but it may negatively affect learning. Cooper, Heron, and Heward (1987) listed questions that should be asked prior to the start of a behavior change program. These questions can be summarized into the following:

1. Does the behavior disrupt learning?
2. Does the behavior seem to trigger other problem behaviors?
3. Does the behavior result in the exclusion of the individual socially or academically?

Affirmative answers to these questions indicate that the behavior is negatively affecting the student academically or socially and that a formal behavior change plan may be needed. The development and implementation of behavior programs is an expensive proposition in terms of time and effort. In addition, the possible stigma associated with a formal behavior program may follow a child for some time. We must take measures to ensure that these resources are used correctly and wisely.

Step 2: Define the Behavior To Change

Once you have determined that the behavior is important and warrants a formal behavior change plan, you should move on to the second step, which is formally defining the behavior to change. A good definition of behavior serves three purposes. First, objective definitions provide practitioners with a behavior to target. Specific behaviors lead to specific interventions. Take Michael for example. Michael's teacher, Ms. M, often complains that he engages in inappropriate behavior. *Inappropriate behavior* is a very broad term that could mean just about anything (e.g., hitting others, cursing, cutting in the lunch line, failing to complete homework assignments on time). Each of the preceding examples of inappropriate behaviors may be linked to a very specific intervention. For example, students who cut in the lunch line may be asked to go to the back of the line. Students who fail to complete their homework may be given rewards for homework completion. Interventions that are focused on a specific behavior are often more effective than a "one size fits all" approach.

Second, well-constructed definitions help ensure that the program will be implemented the same way across settings and intervenors. In other words, objectively defined behaviors keep all persons involved in the behavior change plan on the same page. Imagine the results if all of Michael's teachers implemented an intervention for inappropriate behavior. They could end up with 10 different interventions for 10 different behaviors. Terms such as *inappropriate behavior* leave too much room for interpretation. Parents and teachers have their own levels of tolerance and corresponding ideas of what constitutes inappropriate behavior. Although diversity of opinion is welcomed, differences in definitions of behaviors can lead to ineffective behavior change programs.

Finally, objective definitions allow practitioners to measure the same behavior over and over. At some point you will need to determine if your intervention is effective. The main question is whether the behavior is moving in the right direction. The most efficient way to determine efficacy is to count the number of times a behavior happens before the intervention, and then count the number of times the behavior happens during intervention. Target behaviors that are not well defined result in data that are inaccurate. The main problem with inaccurate data is that any decision you make regarding the program (e.g., when to stop the program or change the intervention) is somewhat suspect. Think about the consequences if your physician used a thermometer that registered a different temperature with each reading. Would this thermometer be useful in determining the effects of an antibiotic on your fever? The physician would never know whether your fever was decreasing as a result of the antibiotic or the change was a result of a faulty reading. Any decision regarding course of treatment (e.g., changing dosage or type of antibiotic) could be wrong. Monitoring behavior change programs works in a similar manner. If your definition of behavior is open to interpretation, any differences in responding could be attributed to an inaccurate measurement system, which could affect any subsequent decisions regarding the program.

So, how do you develop a good definition of behavior? Focus on what the student does, or what you want the student to do. Too often we describe behavior as what we think the student *is* instead of what the student *does*. For example, you may have listened while parents or teachers describe students as being funny, smart, hyperactive, or sneaky. Unfortunately, these adjectives tell us little about the behaviors in which the students engage that make us believe they are funny, smart, hyperactive, or sneaky. Good definitions of behavior describe the how: How do we know that a student is funny, smart, hyperactive, or sneaky? Teachers may know Mary is funny because she tells jokes that make others laugh. Greg is smart because he correctly reads 100 words per minute. Sydney is hyperactive because she is out of her seat for 30 minutes of the 40-minute class. Sally is sneaky because she takes objects without permission. If you asked 10 teachers to observe Sally at the same time and count the number of times she took an object without permission you would get very similar results. However, if you asked those same teachers to count the number of times Sally was "sneaky," you would probably get very different results.

The bottom line is that behaviors should be observable and measurable. That is, you should be able to see and count the behaviors. What sets a good definition apart from a poor definition is that everyone involved in the program should be able to accurately count the behaviors and get the same results.

▶ **Assignment:** Write an observable and measurable behavior for each statement.

1. Is punctual _____

2. Is intelligent _____

3. Has tantrums _____

4. Is hostile _____

Step 3: Collect Baseline Data

The third step of developing a behavior change plan is to collect baseline data. *Baseline data* provide information about the behavior and are collected prior to intervention. Baseline data serve at least two purposes. First, they allow us to confirm that a behavior problem occurs consistently and at levels that warrant a formal plan. In Step 1, we talked about making sure the potential behavior change is important to the student. Collecting baseline data helps further validate the need for a program. Problem behaviors that occur often and at high levels probably require more attention than those that occur occasionally.

Second, baseline data give a comparison for intervention. Without baseline data we have no way of gauging the effectiveness of our new program. Baseline data tell the story of the behavior prior to intervention. In comparing data from before and after the intervention we can decide if our program significantly benefited the student. Baseline data maximize the effects of our programs by allowing for fast changes in interventions as needed. To collect baseline data, document the number of times (or how long) a behavior occurs for several days prior to intervention. These data will then provide the comparison to evaluate the next step in program development: implementing the program.

Step 4: Implement the Program

The fourth step of a behavior change program is to implement the actual program. The program typically consists of interventions developed from the principles discussed earlier in this book (e.g., positive reinforcement, punishment). Interested readers are also referred to the *How To Improve Classroom Behavior* series (published by PRO-ED) for a more detailed examination of techniques to deal with specific problem behaviors.

When implementing behavioral interventions, consider the four factors that tend to make the difference between an effective plan and one that fails (Lee, Kubina, & Smith, 2003). First, the intervention must actually be implemented. A well-designed plan on paper that fails to make it to the classroom or home cannot work. This is akin to your mechanic telling you what is wrong with your car and then not fixing it!

Second, the intervention must be consistently implemented. When you are inconsistent with the intervention, you are sending mixed messages to the student. For example, Mr. L has implemented a behavior change program for Maria. However, he is very inconsistent. Sometimes he provides consequences when Maria bullies others, and at other times he does not. As a result, Maria is unsure of the classroom behavior boundaries and tends to push the limits on acceptable behaviors. One of the main reasons for the failure of behavior programs is the inconsistent application of procedures. Teachers should train staff and have written copies of all procedures. Similarly, parents may post the steps of the plan in a visible place, such as the refrigerator, as a reminder. Everyone must be on the same page for the program to work.

Third, you must be patient. Behaviorally based techniques are advantageous because they generally produce long-term behavior change. Unfortunately, these same techniques sometimes take time to work. Changing behavior is not as easy as flipping a light switch. It can be hard work, but the outcomes are invaluable. Once you are sure that the intervention is being implemented appropriately, give it a chance to work.

Finally, the intervention plan must be easy to implement. We have spoken with teachers who have developed the most theoretically sound programs but never could never use those programs in real settings because of their complexity. In many cases several people will be implementing the behavior plan. A good rule of thumb is to set the level of complexity so that the person with the least amount of skill and training can use the plan effectively.

One additional factor that could be added to the description of a successful program is "buy in." Parents and professionals who have a vested interest in the success of a program tend to implement that program more effectively than people who are forced to use a program. Be sure to get input from all parties involved before starting a formal behavior program. Each person has something different to bring to the table in terms of experiences and expertise. Your job is to bring out those abilities to effect desirable changes in behavior.

Step 5: Collect Data on the Effects of the Program and Make Necessary Changes

One key thing to remember in developing behavior or academic plans for children is that there are no "do overs" or "mulligans." The children with whom we deal have real problems that prevent them from achieving their academic and social potential. We can ill afford to use ineffective interventions. As teachers and parents, our mistakes follow children for the rest of their lives. The problem is not so much with the ineffective intervention. Our imperfect world includes interventions that do not work. The problem occurs when practitioners continue to use the ineffective intervention. Data collection allows you to quickly determine if an intervention is working as planned. A simple way to evaluate the effectiveness of your behavior program is to keep track of how often the target behavior occurs during the intervention and then to compare those numbers to baseline data. If the behavior is going in the right direction, give yourself a pat on the back—good job! However, if the behavior is not changing as planned, go back and modify the intervention and continue the process of evaluation.

Basic Principles Quiz 12

1. List the five steps for developing a behavior change program.

    a. _____

    b. _____

    c. _____

    d. _____

    e. _____

2. What are three questions you should consider when targeting a behavior for change?

    a. _____

    b. _____

    c. _____

3. Name three reasons why objective definitions are important.

    a. _____

    _____

    b. _____

    _____

    c. _____

    _____

4. Define *baseline data*.

    _____

    _____

_____

_____

_____

5. Name five factors that can make the difference between an effective and an ineffective behavior change plan.

a. _____

b. _____

c. _____

d. _____

e. _____

Assumptions About Changing Behavior

In addition to the basic steps of behavior change, Lee, Kubina, and Smith (2003) listed several assumptions that should guide behavior change programs. When combined with basic behavior principles and steps of behavior change, these assumptions help set the stage for effective interventions.

Assumption 1: Data-Based Approaches Are Generally More Effective than Shotgun Approaches

In a data-based approach, practitioners use information about the setting and behavior to develop a plan to address each individual behavior. In contrast, with a shotgun approach, practitioners use one or two blanket approaches to manage all behaviors. The comparison of data-based and shotgun approaches is similar to the difference between using a sprinkler system or using a watering can to water a flower. The sprinkler system certainly spreads out a great deal of water, only some of which may actually hit the flower. In fact, the system may provide only the bare minimum amount of water needed to sustain the flower. To provide the water necessary for the flower to grow, the sprinkler system would need to stay on many hours, spreading hundreds of gallons of water across a large area. A watering can, however, can be used to deliver water where the plant needs it, at the roots. The watering can is more efficient and more effective than a large sprinkler system when you're watering a single flower. Data-based approaches are similar to the watering can in that they enable practitioners to develop interventions that are very specific and get at the root of a problem.

Unfortunately, practitioners too often subscribe to the shotgun method when selecting interventions and use one or two interventions for every infraction of the rules. These blanket approaches may not always be effective, as shown in the following example. Rich and George seem to constantly use foul language in Ms. T's classroom. True to form, Ms. T gives both students time-out when they curse. She has collected the following data on instances of swearing. As shown in Figure 10, the intervention seemed to work well for Rich but actually increased George's cursing behavior. This "one size fits all" approach for assigning time out was obviously ineffective.

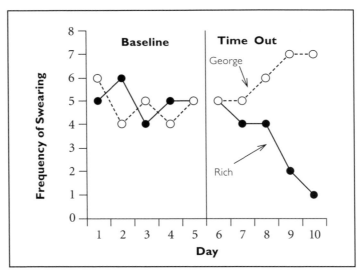

Figure 10. The results of Ms. T's time-out intervention for swearing.

How could data be used to improve this situation? Ms. T could have increased the chances of success by collecting data on the events that occurred before and after each episode of cursing. One systematic method of collecting these data, called *functional assessment,* seeks to determine why a person engages in a particular behavior. In a functional assessment, practitioners observe the events that precede and follow a behavior in order to determine events that trigger and maintain that behavior. Functional assessment is based on the premise that behavior is contextual and serves a purpose for an individual. In other words, behavior does not occur in a vacuum. Behavior occurs because of environmental events and is maintained by events in that environment. In general, the function, or purpose, of behavior is to obtain (e.g., attention, objects) or avoid (e.g., a person, academic assignments) stimuli. Consider the child who cried at the supermarket checkout at the start of this book. The antecedent stimulus that triggered the tantrum was the presence of candy at the checkout. In this case the purpose of crying was most likely to obtain candy. Knowledge of the function of behavior allows parents and practitioners to develop interventions that are geared toward preventing problem behavior by modifying the antecedents associated with the behavior or replacing the inappropriate behavior with a more acceptable alternative that serves the same purpose. In the checkout example, the parent could either (a) modify the antecedents by going through a checkout line that does not have candy or (b) teach the child a more appropriate way to ask for candy. The frequency of candy purchasing could then be reduced over time, thus thinning the schedule of reinforcement for appropriate requesting behavior.

Functional assessment can be a complicated and time-consuming process. However, there is a streamlined version, called an *ABC analysis,* that parents and practitioners can use to help determine antecedents and consequences of behavior. In an ABC analysis, an observer first writes down everything that happens to the student during several observation periods when the inappropriate behavior is likely to occur. The observer then uses a table, like the one shown in Figure 11, to organize the events based on antecedents, behaviors, and consequences. To analyze the data, the observer looks for patterns of antecedents and consequences. Once a pattern is established, the practitioner can develop an intervention based on the information.

In the example of Rich and George, Ms. T decided to collect ABC data on both students. The first step was to observe the target students and write down everything that happened in the setting. This type of data collection is called *anecdotal data* or *narrative recording*. The main focus of the narrative should be on the events that come before and after the target behavior (i.e., antecedents and consequences). Here is a sample of the narrative Ms. T wrote during the first few days of observation:

> **Monday (math class)**—Rich curses at another student when entering the room. Teacher ignores this behavior. Rich then repeats the curse word louder. Teacher tells Rich to sit down on his chair. Students are asked to complete independent math activity. George says, "I'm not doing this #*&^% work."

Antecedent	Behavior	Consequence

Figure 11. Sample ABC recording form.

Teacher asks George to begin working. George completes one problem incorrectly.

Tuesday (social studies class)—Rich curses during group activity. Teacher verbally reprimands Rich. Later in that same class, Rich curses when he drops his pencil. Teacher asks Rich to sit next to her desk.

Tuesday (math class)—Students are given a worksheet to review previous day's work. Rich, sitting next to Teacher's desk, completes paper. George pushes paper off desk and swears. Teacher gives verbal reprimand. George does not finish paper.

Wednesday (social studies class)—Class discusses ancient Egypt. Rich curses in middle of discussion. Other students laugh. Teacher reprimands Rich. Later in the class, Rich puts his head down and mumbles a few curse words. Teacher asks Rich to take a seat next to her desk.

Wednesday (math class)—Students are asked to pull out homework assignments. George makes an inappropriate comment about homework ("I hate &$#@ homework"). Teacher says, "George, I have had it with you. Go and sit in the back of the room."

Narratives are useful tools to collect a great deal of data. However, it can be difficult to make sense of the data because the events are in paragraph form. An ABC recording form, like the one shown in Figures 12 and 13, can help Ms. T discover more discernable patterns of antecedents and consequences.

Armed with this knowledge of antecedents and consequences of cursing, Ms. T can develop a program that is tailored to meet the needs of each individual student. In this case, the data (see Figure 10) suggest that time out was effective for Rich, indicating that something in the time-in environment was reinforcing. ABC data revealed that teacher attention or laughter from peers probably helped maintain cursing behavior. Eliminating this source of reinforcement through time out quickly reduced the cursing behavior. On the other hand, George's

Antecedent	Behavior	Consequence
Rich enters room (math).	Rich curses.	Teacher ignores behavior.
Teacher ignores behavior.	Rich curses louder.	Teacher tells Rich to sit in his chair.
Group engages in activity.	Rich curses.	Teacher gives verbal reprimand.
Rich drops pencil.	Rich curses.	Teacher asks Rich to sit next to Teacher's desk.
Rich sits next to Teacher.	Rich completes work.	
Class participates in discussion.	Rich curses.	Students laugh and Teacher reprimands.
Class participates in discussion.	Rich mumbles curse words.	Rich is asked to move his desk next to Teacher's desk.

Figure 12. ABC recording form for Rich.

swearing increased (see Figure 10) when the time-out intervention was implemented, indicating that avoiding or escaping the assignment actually was reinforcing. An ABC analysis of the classroom setting revealed a possible source of aversion. George seemed to swear more often when math assignments were given. He has learned that one easy way to save face and not have to ask for assistance is to curse during class because the teacher asks him to leave the room. In this case Ms. T can modify the assignment by making sure that the task is not too difficult for George, using high-p request sequences embedded in the task, or delivering reinforcers for task completion.

Assumption 2: Positive Approaches Can Be More Effective Than Aversive Approaches in the Long Term

Unfortunately, aversive approaches to behavior change seem to be the norm in homes and schools. More aversive approaches

Antecedent	Behavior	Consequence
Students are given math work.	George curses.	Teacher asks George to complete work.
Teacher asks George to complete work.	George completes one problem incorrectly.	
Group reviews math worksheet.	George pushes paper off desk and curses.	Teacher gives verbal reprimand. Paper is not completed.
Students are asked to take out homework.	George makes inappropriate comment about homework.	George is asked to sit in back of room.

Figure 13. ABC recording form for George.

can be very effective at reducing problem behavior in the short term. However, practitioners and parents should be aware of the following drawbacks regarding aversive approaches.

First, it is difficult to teach appropriate behavior using aversive approaches. These techniques are designed to reduce a problem behavior. Unfortunately, they do not teach a new adaptive behavior. For example, giving Rich (from our earlier example) a time out reduced his cursing behavior. However, the use of time out did not promote a new, more appropriate behavior. A better program would use time out to reduce cursing and systematic reinforcement to increase an appropriate behavior, such as raising his hand to attract teacher attention.

Second, aversive techniques can create friction between the child and the behavior change agent. In a classroom setting, many students who require more formalized behavior plans have a history of being unsuccessful in school. This lack of success already makes the school environment somewhat aversive. As teachers and parents, we do not want to perpetuate this aversion.

Third, the immediate effects of aversive techniques on student behavior often negatively reinforce the behavior of using those same approaches. For example, Mr. P finds that yelling at students is an effective way to quiet his classroom. Mr. P will probably continue to yell in similar situations because each time he yells the students quiet down. From Mr. P's standpoint, there is no need to use a positive approach because the aversive approach is effective, at least temporarily. However, Mr. P should be aware that students might begin to associate him and the class with aversive consequences. Again, we do not want to perpetuate aversive school environments.

Finally, we need to remember that our interventions are a powerful model for students. Do we want our children handling every situation using aversive consequences? What have the students learned from Mr. P? Yelling works! They have not learned about more positive ways to gain attention. We must be careful to select procedures that are effective and provide good examples. We are not saying that aversive techniques should be eliminated from your repertoire. They certainly are effective and have their place. We are saying that a balanced approach is probably best.

Assumption 3: Teaching Students To Manage Their Own Behavior Is More Efficient Than Methods That Require Constant Teacher Attention

The ultimate goal of any teaching approach, whether it is implemented by teachers or parents, is to have children perform the new behaviors we teach in other settings. In other words, we want the behavior to generalize. When we develop behavior programs, this becomes a major issue. We have often heard teachers complain that programs may help students behave appropriately in one setting, but the effects don't "spill over" to other areas. This lack of generalization is essentially an issue of stimulus control. The student responds appropriately in the presence of stimuli associated with the formal management program (e.g., the teacher, the data sheets, the reinforcers).

When those stimuli are no longer present, however, the student reverts to inappropriate behavior. What is needed is a technique that bridges the gap between the stimuli associated with the formal program and other environments. Self-management strategies provide such a bridge.

Hughes, Therrien, and Lee (2004) defined *behavioral self-management* as the personal application of behavior change strategies in order to change behavior. Overall, self-management strategies have been shown to be effective across social and academic areas and across a variety of students. There are two general forms of behavioral self-management.

The first and probably simplest form of self-management entails using prompts to make certain aspects of the environment more salient in order to remember needed items or events. For example, writing a list before you go to the grocery store or placing your umbrella next to the door so that you won't forget it in the morning are two examples of this type of self-management. In both of these examples, certain aspects of the environment were made more salient, increasing the likelihood that a behavior will occur. These changes can be low-tech (e.g., paper and pencil) or more high-tech. Technology such as personal data assistants (PDAs) now make organizing anything from grocery lists to homework assignments easy.

A second type of self-management relies on people to observe and record their behavior, evaluate its quality, and deliver contingent consequences. An individual can implement this type of self-management in five steps:

1. Define the behavior to self-monitor.
2. Count the number of times the behavior occurs.
3. Graph the resulting data each day or each week.
4. Set goals for increasing or decreasing the target behavior.
5. Deliver consequences.

We can apply this system of self-management to Caleb, a student who fails to complete his homework assignments on time. His teacher, Mr. Z, first helps Caleb define homework completion (e.g., finishing at least 90% of a given assignment and turning it in on the due date). Next, Caleb is taught to keep track of the number of times the behavior occurs. He uses a data sheet similar to the one shown in Figure 14.

After collecting a week's worth of data, Caleb begins to graph the data. Graphing the data makes it very easy to determine progress (see Figure 15).

At the weekly graphing sessions, Caleb and Mr. Z. set goals for homework completion. During the first 3 weeks of the self-management program (Weeks 5–7 on the graph), Caleb completed an average of 50% of homework assignments. For the 4th week of intervention, Caleb and Mr. Z decide to set a goal of 75% of assignments completed. Finally, a reward is delivered if Caleb meets the agreed-upon goal. The goal will be increased every week or so until Caleb is completing homework at the same percentage as his peers. Mr. Z can also combine the self-observation method of management with self-prompting by asking Caleb to write down assignments using a homework planner or PDA.

	Caleb's Homework Completion					
	Monday	**Tuesday**	**Wednesday**	**Thursday**	**Friday**	**Weekly Totals**
Number Assigned	|||	||	|||	||	|||	13
Number Completed	||	||	|||	0	|	8
				Percentage Completed		62%

Figure 14. Self-management data sheet for Caleb.

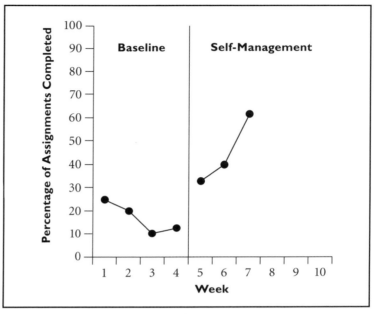

Figure 15. Caleb's homework completion.

Basic Principles Quiz 13

1. What is a data-based approach to program development?

_____

_____

_____

_____

_____

_____

2. What does an ABC analysis tell?

_____

_____

_____

_____

3. Name two functions of behavior.

   a. _____

   b. _____

4. What are two disadvantages of aversive approaches?

   a. _____

   _____

   b. _____

   _____

5. Name two major approaches to self-management.

   a. _____

   b. _____

SUMMARY AND CONCLUSIONS

Throughout this book we have discussed some basic principles of behavior. Each of the principles and techniques presented has solid research support as a method to modify behavior. However, as we tell our students, "Don't believe me. Go and check out the research literature for yourself." You may think that your behavioral issue is unique. Nine times out of 10, however, someone, somewhere has published research on a program for that very problem. Use the literature! Do not let this book be the end of your exploration of behavior.

We hope that this book has helped increase your understanding of how and why behavior occurs. Often, when people think about behavior modification, they conjure Orwellian images of a controlling Big Brother. However, as you have probably ascertained by now, the term *behavior modification* is somewhat of a misnomer. People do not directly modify behavior. The environment modifies behavior. We simply arrange the environment to make behavior more or less likely. It is through these arrangements that we can create meaningful opportunities for all people.

FINAL EXAMINATION

1. Define *reinforcement.*

   _____

   _____

   _____

   _____

   _____

2. To maximize the effectiveness of a reinforcement procedure, the following three conditions must be met:

   a. _____

   _____

   b. _____

   _____

   c. _____

   _____

3. How are positive reinforcement and negative reinforcement similar?

   _____

   _____

4. How are positive reinforcement and negative reinforcement different?

   _____

   _____

   _____

_____

_____

5. Distinguish between a primary reinforcer and a secondary reinforcer.

_____

_____

_____

_____

_____

6. Define *deprivation* and *satiation*.

_____

_____

_____

_____

_____

7. Why would it be best to use a continuous reinforcement schedule when reinforcing a new behavior?

_____

_____

_____

_____

_____

8. Once a behavior is established, what kind of reinforcement schedule should be used to maintain the behavior? Why?

_____

_____

_____

_____

_____

9. Describe the ABCs model of behavior. Give three examples of how this model may operate in a home.

_____

_____

_____

_____

_____

10. What is the difference between an S^D and an S^Δ?

_____

_____

_____

_____

_____

11. Suppose the expression "Well done" is not a social reinforcer for someone. Indicate how you could make the expression into a social reinforcer.

_____

_____

_____

_____

_____

12. Schools are already using a token reinforcement system: student grades. Why is this token system so often ineffective?

_____

_____

_____

_____

_____

Fred was a 17-year-old junior in high school. He frequently skipped classes and was receiving Ds and Fs in all his classes except for gym. He was also argumentative at home. He frequently shouted at his parents and claimed that they did not give him enough allowance or access to the car, even though his parents owned two cars. He also objected because his mother nagged him about how he was doing in school, keeping his room clean, and coming in on time. The school counselor tried setting up a program whereby Fred could earn privileges, such as going to assemblies or visiting the student lounge, for going to class or getting good grades. However, Fred did not respond to the program but instead continued to skip classes other than gym. He frequently disappeared to play video games at a shopping mall or basketball at an outdoor court in a nearby playground.

13. Suggest a reinforcer sampling procedure the parents might use to increase the probability that Fred will respond to a reinforcer they might offer.

_____

_____

_____

_____

_____

14. List four considerations that could help a new teacher or a parent more effectively deliver verbal praise.

    a. _____

    b. _____

    c. _____

    d. _____

15. What is a contingency contract? What are some rules for a well-written contract?

    _____

    _____

    _____

    _____

    _____

16. Describe a shaping procedure for a student who could only sit still for 2 minutes in an hour. The desired terminal behavior is to sit still for 20 minutes.

    _____

    _____

    _____

    _____

    _____

17. What is instructional control? How is it established?

    _____

_____

_____

_____

_____

18. Describe three factors that increase the probability that a modeled behavior will be imitated.

_____

_____

_____

_____

_____

19. Distinguish among forward chaining, backward chaining, and total task presentation.

_____

_____

_____

_____

_____

20. Mark is a child who constantly irritates his mother until she gets angry with him. Mom suspects that the attention she gives to Mark is reinforcing the behavior. She therefore tries to extinguish the behavior by ignoring Mark's irritating comments. What are three things that Mark's mother should expect to happen?

_____

_____

_____

_____

21. How are negative reinforcement and punishment different? Give an example of each procedure.

_____

_____

_____

_____

_____

22. List the five steps of behavior change.

  a. _____

  b. _____

  c. _____

  d. _____

  e. _____

23. What are three questions you should consider when targeting a behavior for change?

  a. _____

  b. _____

  c. _____

24. Name five factors that can make the difference between an effective and an ineffective behavior change plan.

  a. _____

  b. _____

  c. _____

d. _____

e. _____

25. What is a data-based approach to program development?

_____

_____

_____

_____

_____

ANSWERS TO BASIC PRINCIPLES QUIZZES AND FINAL EXAMINATION

Basic Principles Quiz I

1. A stimulus is any object or event in the environment that can change behavior.

2. Precede.

3. Respondent behaviors are involuntary and operant behaviors are voluntary. Respondent behaviors are elicited, whereas operant behaviors are emitted.

4. Elicits the response.

5. Without the unconditioned stimulus.

6. The stimuli that elicit strong undesirable emotional responses should not be paired with school.

7. Operant conditioning is the process by which the consequences of behavior change the future rate of that behavior. Answers to the second part of the question will vary.

8. Reinforcement is the process by which the consequences of a behavior increase the future rate of that behavior.

9. a. The reinforcer should immediately follow the appropriate behavior.
   b. The reinforcer should be delivered contingent on the desired behavior.
   c. Reinforcers should be varied.

10. Answers will vary.

11. The data are not an example of reinforcement because no increase in behavior was observed.

Basic Principles Quiz 2

1. Negative reinforcement. Mindy stops crying when her father picks her up, increasing the probability that her father will pick her up the next time she cries.

2. Mike is positively reinforcing Mindy's crying. He gives her something she wants when she cries and she will continue to cry in the future.

3. They both produce an increase in responding.

4. With positive reinforcement a person receives something she wants. With negative reinforcement she gets rid of something she dislikes.

5. Negative reinforcement occurred. Holly was removed from a situation, and an increase in behavior was observed.

Basic Principles Quiz 3

1. A primary reinforcer does not depend on previous conditioning for its reinforcing power. A secondary reinforcer does depend on previous conditioning.

2. Answers will vary.

3. By pairing the smiley face with another reinforcer.

4. Answers will vary.

5. Because money can be used to purchase a large variety of other reinforcers.

6. Deprivation occurs when an individual has not had access to a specific reinforcer and as a result desires that reinforcer. Satiation occurs when a person has had access to a reinforcer for some time and as a result no longer desires that reinforcer.

Basic Principles Quiz 4

1. Continuous reinforcement schedules increase the number of learning trials for a behavior during a fixed period and result in quicker acquisition of that behavior.

2. Because with ratio schedules, the more a person responds correctly, the more often she or he acquires reinforcers. With interval schedules, responding before the interval has passed is wasted effort.

3. One of the intermittent schedules of reinforcement should be used because it produces more durable behavior than a continuous schedule.

4. One example would be reinforcers that are separated by 3, 22, 9, 8, 27, 21 responses (note that the average of these numbers is 15). Any other series of numbers that averages 15 is also correct.

Basic Principles Quiz 5

1. A = Antecedent, B = Behavior, and C = Consequences. Answers to the second part will vary.

2. Behavior that is under stimulus control only occurs under very specific environmental conditions (stimuli). Answers to the second part will vary.

3. An S^D signals that reinforcement is available for a behavior. An S^Δ signals that reinforcement is not available.

4. The process works exactly the same for both appropriate and inappropriate behavior. A stimulus serves as a signal that reinforcement is available for a behavior (appropriate or inappropriate).

Basic Principles Quiz 6

1. Answers will vary.

2. By pairing it with an established reinforcer.

3. Because it is exchangeable for fewer back-up reinforcers (i.e., it is a less generalized reinforcer).

4. Answers will vary.

5. Because grades are delivered long after relevant behaviors occur and because there is no systematic relationship between grades and back-up reinforcers.

6. The advantages of token systems: They are nondisruptive, are associated with many reinforcers, can be delivered immediately, provide immediate feedback, allow for graded reinforcement, allow for unusual or expensive reinforcers, help in setting goals, teach people to delay reinforcement, and

are powerful. The disadvantages of token systems are that implementation is sometimes cumbersome and they can be expensive.

Basic Principles Quiz 7

1. Apparently the consequences the counselor offered Fred were not reinforcers for his behavior.

2. An increased allowance, driving privileges, playing arcade games, and playing basketball.

3. Answers will vary.

4. Let him drive the car to school for a day or two. Tell him he can earn more days to use the car by keeping his room clean. Increase his allowance for one week and tell him he can have a permanent increase in his allowance if his behavior improves.

Basic Principles Quiz 8

1. A contingency contract is a written agreement between at least two parties specifying the reinforcers one person will provide to the other for meeting specified goals. A well-written contract should emphasize the desired rather than the undesired behaviors; provide small rewards for reasonable improvement; provide short-term rewards; be clear; and be adjusted gradually as improvement occurs.

2. Answers will vary but should include some of the following:
   a. Make praise contingent on appropriate behavior.
   b. Make praise sound and be sincere.
   c. When giving social reinforcers, learn to smile, give eye contact, and ask questions about what the other person says.
   d. Pair social reinforcement with other reinforcers by lending a helping hand or giving other reinforcers with a smile and a word of praise.
   e. Become skilled at private, indirect, and public praise.
   f. Use social reinforcement in conjunction with other available reinforcers.
   g. Learn to be specific in your praise.

3. Answers will vary. However, the basic idea is to present a series of three or four brief requests with a high probability of compliance just prior to the request to transition to the new activity.

Basic Principles Quiz 9

1. Answers will vary. However, the basic idea is to systematically increase the requirements for a reinforcer from 2 minutes to 20 minutes.

2. Answers will vary.

3. Answers will vary.

4. To motivate behavior and provide feedback on the quality or quantity of past behaviors.

5. Instructional control describes a situation in which a mentor gives an instruction and the learner follows the instruction. Instructional control is established by reinforcing behaviors that comply with the instruction.

Basic Principles Quiz 10

1. A behavior is more likely to be imitated if the model's behavior is reinforced, particularly with large amounts of reinforcement; if the behavior is simple; and if the model is similar to the learner in terms of gender, race, and age.

2. In forward chaining, the first link in the chain is taught first, followed by the second link, and so forth. In backward chaining, the last link is taught first, followed by the next-to-last link, and so forth. Total task presentation involves presenting each step of the task for every instructional trial.

3. Shaping involves teaching a new behavior. Fading involves getting an existing behavior to occur in a new situation. In shaping, what the learner does changes. In fading, what the teacher does changes. Shaping involves manipulating consequences. Fading involves changing antecedents.

4. Instructional control.

5. She pulled back on the control column instead of the throttle.

6. S^D.

7. No (only partially).

8. Prompting and fading.

9. a. To discriminate the throttle from the control column.

   b. That "easing back" meant pulling back slowly rather than suddenly on the throttle.

10.

S^D	R (Response)	S^D (Reinforcer)	R (Response)	Reinforcer or S^D (Reinforcer)
"Ease back"	Looks toward throttle	Sees throttle		
	Reaches for throttle	Feels throttle	Grasps throttle	
		Feels throttle	Pulls back throttle	Feels throttle
			Stops throttle	Hears engine pitch change; instructor says, "Great!"

(Any of these, plus other components, are possible.)

Basic Principles Quiz II

1. Level 1—Differential reinforcement (DRO, DRL, DRI, DRA)
   Level 2—Extinction
   Level 3—Removal of desirables (response cost, time out)
   Level 4—Presentation of aversives (reprimands)
   Specific examples will vary.

2. The behavior will decrease slowly. It might occur more frequently before decreasing in rate. It might spontaneously occur again after it has apparently been extinguished.

3. Resistance to extinction is the number of responses that occurs once reinforcement is terminated. Any of the intermittent schedules of reinforcement will produce resistance to extinction. VI schedules will produce the greatest resistance because they program reinforcement in the most unpredictable manner.

4. A DRL schedule provides reinforcement if a person's or group's behavior occurs below a certain rate. You could set the criterion at slightly below the rate that occurred during baseline.

5. Extinction involves withholding a reinforcer to eliminate a behavior. Punishment is the process by which the consequences of a behavior reduce the probability that a given behavior will occur in the future. Extinction and punishment both produce a decrease in behavior. Extinction involves the termination of a consequence for a behavior. Punishment generally involves the presentation of a consequence for a behavior.

6. Negative reinforcement results in an increase in the behavior. Punishment results in a decrease. Answers to the second part will vary.

7. The punishing stimulus should be intense, it should immediately follow the behavior, and it should be combined with positive reinforcement for appropriate behavior.

8. Reinforcement is important because it teaches the correct behavior. It results in a quicker and greater reduction in the undesired behavior. It allows for the use of a less intense punisher. It reduces some of the adverse side effects of punishment. Descriptions of specific programs will vary.

9. Answers will vary but should include an urgent need to reduce the occurrence of the behavior and failed attempts to use only positive reinforcement.

10. The data show a decrease in assignment completion contingent on verbal praise. Therefore, verbal praise is a punisher.

Basic Principles Quiz 12

1. The five steps for developing a behavior change program:
   a. Identify the behavior targeted for intervention.
   b. Define the behavior to change.
   c. Collect baseline data.
   d. Implement the program.
   e. Collect data on the effects of the program and make necessary changes.

2. a. Does the behavior disrupt learning?
   b. Does the behavior seem to trigger other problem behaviors?

c. Does the behavior result in the exclusion of the individual (socially or academically)?

3. First, objective definitions provide practitioners with a behavior to target. Second, well-constructed definitions help ensure that the program will be implemented the same way across settings and intervenors. Finally, objective definitions enable practitioners to measure the same behavior over and over.

4. Baseline data are data collected prior to the start of an intervention.

5. a. The intervention must actually be implemented.

   b. The intervention must be consistently implemented.

   c. You must be patient.

   d. The intervention plan must be easy to implement.

   e. Those involved must have a vested interested in the success of the program (i.e., buy in).

Basic Principles Quiz 13

1. A data-based approach uses data to determine the function of the target behavior and uses that information to develop a very specific intervention.

2. An ABC analysis gives information about the context of behavior. More specifically, ABC analyses give information about the antecedents that trigger behavior and consequences that maintain that behavior.

3. Get or obtain; avoid or escape.

4. Answers may vary, but should include two of the following:

   a. It is difficult to teach appropriate behavior using aversive approaches.

   b. Aversive techniques can create friction between the child and the behavior change agent.

   c. The immediate effects of aversive techniques on student behavior often reinforce the behavior of those carrying out the aversive approach.

   d. We may not want to model aversive interventions for students.

5. a. Using prompts to make certain aspects of the environment more salient.

   b. Self-recording behavior.

Answers to Final Examination

1. Reinforcement is the process by which the consequences of a behavior increase the future rate of that behavior.

2. a. The reinforcer should immediately follow the appropriate behavior.
   b. The reinforcer should be delivered contingent on the desired behavior.
   c. Reinforcers should be varied.

3. They both produce an increase in responding.

4. With positive reinforcement, a person receives something she or he wants. With negative reinforcement, the person gets rid of something she or he dislikes.

5. A primary reinforcer does not depend on previous conditioning for its reinforcing power. A secondary reinforcer does depend on previous conditioning.

6. Deprivation occurs when an individual has not had access to a specific reinforcer and as a result desires that reinforcer. Satiation occurs when a person has had access to a reinforcer for some time and as a result no longer desires that reinforcer.

7. Continuous reinforcement schedules increase the number of learning trials for a behavior during a fixed period and result in quicker acquisition of that behavior.

8. One of the intermittent schedules of reinforcement should be used because it produces more durable behavior than a continuous schedule.

9. A = Antecedent, B = Behavior, and C = Consequences. Answers to the second part will vary.

10. An S^D signals that reinforcement is available for a behavior. An S^Δ signals that reinforcement is not available.

11. By pairing it with an established reinforcer.

12. Because grades are delivered long after relevant behaviors occur and because there is no systematic relationship between grades and back-up reinforcers.

13. Let him drive the car to school for a day or two. Tell him he can earn more days to use the car by keeping his room clean. Increase his allowance for one week and tell him he can have a permanent increase in his allowance if his behavior improves.

14. Answers will vary but should include some of the following:
    a. Make praise contingent on appropriate behavior.
    b. Make praise sound and be sincere.
    c. When giving social reinforcers, learn to smile, give eye contact, and ask questions about what the other person says.
    d. Pair social reinforcement with other reinforcers by lending a helping hand or giving other reinforcers with a smile and a word of praise.
    e. Become skilled at private, indirect, and public praise.
    f. Use social reinforcement in conjunction with other available reinforcers.
    g. Learn to be specific in your praise.

15. A contingency contract is a written agreement between at least two parties specifying the reinforcers one person will provide to the other for meeting specified goals. A well-written contract should emphasize the desired rather than the undesired behaviors; provide small rewards for reasonable improvement; provide short-term rewards; be clear; and be adjusted gradually as improvement occurs.

16. Answers will vary. However, the basic idea is to systematically increase the requirements for a reinforcer from 2 minutes to 20 minutes.

17. Instructional control describes a situation in which a mentor gives an instruction and the learner follows the instruction. It is established by reinforcing behaviors that comply with the instruction.

18. A behavior is more likely to be imitated if the model's behavior is reinforced, particularly with large amounts of reinforcement; if the behavior is simple; and if the model is similar to the learner in terms of gender, race, and age.

19. In forward chaining, the first link in the chain is taught first, followed by the second link, and so forth. In backward chaining, the last link is taught first, followed by the next-to-last link, and so forth. Total task presentation involves presenting each step of the task for every instructional trial.

20. The behavior will decrease slowly. It might occur more frequently before decreasing in rate. It might spontaneously occur again after it has apparently been extinguished.

21. Negative reinforcement results in an increase in the behavior. Punishment results in a decrease. Answers to the second part will vary.

22. The five steps for developing a behavior change program:
    a. Identify the behavior targeted for intervention.
    b. Define the behavior to change.
    c. Collect baseline data.
    d. Implement the program.
    e. Collect data on the effects of the program and make necessary changes.

23. a. Does the behavior disrupt learning?
    b. Does the behavior seem to trigger other problem behaviors?
    c. Does the behavior result in the exclusion of the individual (socially or academically)?

24. a. The intervention must actually be implemented.
    b. The intervention must be consistently implemented.
    c. You must be patient.
    d. The intervention plan must be easy to implement.
    e. Those involved must have a vested interested in the success of the program (i.e., buy in).

25. A data-based approach uses data to determine the function of the target behavior and uses that information to develop a very specific intervention.

REFERENCES AND FURTHER READING

Albers, A. E., & Greer, R. D. (1991). Is the three-term contingency trial a predictor of effective instruction? *Journal of Behavioral Education, 3*, 337–354.

Alberto, P. A., & Troutman, A. C. (2003). *Applied behavior analysis for teachers* (6th ed.). Upper Saddle River, NJ: Merrill Prentice Hall.

Axelrod, S. (1983). *Behavior modification for the classroom teacher.* New York: McGraw-Hill.

Axelrod, S. (1998). *How to use group contingencies.* Austin, TX: PRO-ED.

Axelrod, S. (2003). *How to help students remain seated.* Austin, TX: PRO-ED.

Axelrod, S., & Apsche, J. (Eds.). (1983). *The effects of punishment on human behavior.* New York: Academic Press.

Azrin, N. H., & Holz, W. C. (1966). Punishment. In W. K. Honig (Ed.), *Operant behavior: Areas of research and application* (pp. 380–447). New York: Appleton-Century-Crofts.

Baer, D. M. (1999). *How to plan for generalization* (2nd ed.). Austin, TX: PRO-ED.

Baer, D. M., Wolf, M. M., & Risley, T. R. (1968). Some current dimensions of applied behavior analysis. *Journal of Applied Behavior Analysis, 20*, 313–327.

Cameron, J., Banko, K. M., & Pierce, W. D. (2001). Pervasive negative effects of rewards on intrinsic motivation: The myth continues. *Behavior Analyst, 24*, 1–44.

Carr, E. G., Horner, R. H., Turnbull, A. P., Marquis, J. G., McLaughlin, D. M., McAtee, M. L., et al. (1999). *Positive behavior support for people with developmental disabilities: A research synthesis.* Washington, DC: American Association on Mental Retardation.

Cipani, E. (1998). Three behavioral functions of classroom noncompliance: Diagnostic and treatment implications. *Focus on Autism and Other Developmental Disorders, 13*, 66–72.

Cooper, J., Heron, T., & Heward, W. (1987). *Applied behavior analysis.* Columbus, OH: Merrill.

Demchak, M. (1990). Response prompting and fading methods: A review. *American Journal on Mental Retardation, 94*, 603–615.

deZubicaray, G., & Clair, A. (1998). An evaluation of differential reinforcement of other behavior, differential reinforcement of incompatible behavior, and restitution for the management of aggressive behavior. *Behavioral Interventions, 13*, 157–168.

Frederick, L. D., Deitz, S. M., Bryceland, J. A., & Hummel, J. H. (2000). *Behavior analysis, education, and effective schooling.* Reno, NV: Content Press.

Graff, R. B., & Gibson, L. (2003). Using pictures to assess reinforcers in individuals with developmental disabilities. *Behavior Modification, 27*, 470–483.

Grskovic, J. A., Hall, A. M., Montgomery, D. J., Vargas, A. U., Zentall, S. S., & Belfiore, P. J. (2004). Reducing time-out assignments for students with emotional and behavioral disorders in a self-contained resource classroom. *Journal of Behavioral Education, 13,* 25–36.

Hall, R. V., & Hall, M. L. (1998a). *How to negotiate a behavioral contract* (2nd ed.). Austin, TX: PRO-ED.

Hall, R. V., & Hall, M. L. (1998b). *How to select reinforcers* (2nd ed.). Austin, TX: PRO-ED.

Hall, R. V., & Hall, M. L. (1998c). *How to use planned ignoring (extinction)* (2nd ed.). Austin, TX: PRO-ED.

Hall, R. V., & Hall, M. L. (1998d). *How to use systematic attention and approval* (2nd ed.). Austin, TX: PRO-ED.

Hall, R. V., & Hall, M. L. (1998e). *How to use time out* (2nd ed.). Austin, TX: PRO-ED.

Heward, W. L., Gardner, R., Cavanaugh, R. A., Courson, F. H., Grossi, T. A., & Barbetta, P. M. (1996, Winter). Everyone participates in this class: Using response cards to increase active student response. *Teaching Exceptional Children,* 4–10.

Hughes, C. A., Therrien, W. J., & Lee, D. L. (2004). Effectiveness of behavioral self-management procedures with adolescents with learning and behavior problems. In T. Scruggs & M. Mastropieri (Eds.), *Research in secondary schools: Advances in learning and behavioral disabilities* (Vol. 17, pp. 1–28). Greenwich, CT: JAI Press.

Jenson, W. R., Rhode, G., & Reavis, H. K. (1994–1995). *The tough kid tool box.* Longmont, CO: Sopris West.

Kaplan, J. S., & Carter, J. (1995). *Beyond behavior modification: A cognitive-behavioral approach to behavior management in the school* (3rd ed.). Austin: TX: PRO-ED.

Kazdin, A. E. (2001). *Behavior modification in applied settings* (6th ed.). Belmont, CA: Wadsworth/Thomson Learning.

Kinder, D., & Carnine, D. (1991). Direct instruction: What it is and what it is becoming. *Journal of Behavioral Education, 2,* 192–213.

Kohn, A. (1993). *Punished by rewards: The trouble with gold stars, incentive plans, As, praise, and other bribes.* Boston: Houghton Mifflin.

Lee, D. L. (in press). A quantitative synthesis of applied research on behavioral momentum. *Exceptionality.*

Lee, D. L., & Belfiore, P. J. (1997). Enhancing classroom performance: A review of reinforcement schedules. *Journal of Behavioral Education, 11,* 205–217.

Lee, D. L., Kubina, R. M., & Smith, R. E. (2003). *How to deal effectively with lying, stealing, and cheating.* Austin, TX: PRO-ED.

Lerman, D. C., & Vorndran, C. M. (2002). On the status of knowledge for using punishment: Implications for treating behavior disorders. *Journal of Applied Behavior Analysis, 35,* 431–464.

Lucas, R. L. (2000). The effects of time-out and DRA on the aggressive behavior of a spirited two-year-old. *Child and Family Behavior Therapy, 22*, 51–56.

Luiselli, J. K., & Cameron, M. J. (Eds.). (1998). *Antecedent control: Innovative approaches to behavioral support.* Baltimore: Brookes.

Malott, R. W., Suarez, E. A. T., & Malott, M. E. (2003). *Principles of behavior* (5th ed.). Upper Saddle River, NJ: Pearson/Prentice Hall.

Newsom, C., Favell, J. E., & Rincover, A. (1983). Side effects of punishment. In S. Axelrod & J. Apsche (Eds.), *The effects of punishment on human behavior* (pp. 285–316). New York: Academic Press.

Repp, A. C., & Horner, R. H. (1999). *Functional analysis of problem behavior: From effective assessment to effective support.* Boston: Wadsworth.

Schlosser, R., & Lee, D. L. (2003). Strategies for promoting generalization and maintenance. In R. W. Schlosser (Ed.), *The efficacy of augmentative and alternative communication: Toward evidence-based practice* (pp. 533–552). San Diego, CA: Academic Press.

Schwartz, B. (1978). *Psychology of learning and behavior.* New York: Norton.

Skinner, B. F. (1938). *The behavior of organisms.* Acton, MA: Copley.

Slavin, R. E. (1991). Cooperative learning and group contingencies. *Journal of Behavioral Education, 1*, 105–115.

Sprick, R. S., & Howard, L. (1995). *The teacher's encyclopedia of behavior management: 100 problems/500 plans.* Longmont, CO: Sopris West.

Sterling-Turner, H., & Watson, T. S. (1999). Consultant's guide for the use of time-out in the preschool and elementary classroom. *Psychology in the Schools, 36*, 135–148.

Stokes, T. F., & Baer, D. M. (1977). An implicit technology of generalization. *Journal of Applied Behavior Analysis, 10*, 349–367.

Striefel, S. (1998). *How to teach through modeling and imitation* (2nd ed.). Austin, TX: PRO-ED.

Sugai, G., Horner, R. H., Dunlap, G., Hieneman, M., Lewis, T. J., Nelson, M. C., et al. (2000). Applying positive support and functional behavioral assessment in schools. *Journal of Positive Behavioral Interventions, 2*, 131–143.

Thibadeau, S. F. (1998). *How to use response cost.* Austin, TX: PRO-ED.

Van Houten, R. (1980). *Learning through feedback.* New York: Human Sciences Press.

Van Houten, R. (1998). *How to motivate others through feedback* (2nd ed.). Austin, TX: PRO-ED.

Van Houten, R., & Doleys, D. M. (1983). Are social reprimands effective? In S. Axelrod & J. Apsche (Eds.), *The effects of punishment on human behavior* (pp. 45–70). New York: Academic Press.

Vollmer, T. R. (2002). Punishment happens: Some comments on Lerman and Vorndran's review. *Journal of Applied Behavior Analysis, 35*, 469–473.

Walker, H. M., & Walker, J. E. (1991). *Coping with noncompliance in the classroom: A positive approach for teachers.* Austin, TX: PRO-ED.

Wolery, M., Ault, M. J., & Doyle, P. M. (1992). *Teaching students with moderate to severe disabilities.* New York: Longman.

Zirpoli, T. J. (2004). *Behavior management: Applications for teachers and parents* (4th ed.). Upper Saddle River, NJ: Prentice Hall.

ABOUT THE AUTHORS

David L. Lee is on the special education faculty at Pennsylvania State University. His areas of expertise include assessment and classroom management. Dr. Lee's research focuses on motivational issues in children with attention-deficit/hyperactivity disorder (ADHD) and other behavior disorders. He is currently an associate editor of the *Journal of Behavioral Education*.

Saul Axelrod is professor of special education at Temple University in Philadelphia. His interests include devising and disseminating procedures that increase the academic skills of children living in poverty, and developing techniques for classroom management. He presently serves on the journal editorial boards of *Behavioral Interventions, Behavior Modification,* and *Child and Family Behavior Therapy*. He has written numerous articles and books on applied behavior analysis of a variety of populations and problems.